This book belongs to:

....

DK LONDON
Senior Editor Carrie Love
Publishing Assistant Francesca Harper
Design lead Eleanor Bates
Design by Karen Hood, Hannah Moore, Bhagyashree Nayak, Victoria Palastanga, Lucy Sims, Sadie Thomas
Senior Art Editor Charlotte Bull
Text by Elizabeth Davey, Jonathan Melmoth, Andrea Mills
Subject Consultant Jules Pottle
Illustration by Kitty Glavin, Zishan Mohd
Managing Editor Penny Smith
Production Editor Jacqueline Street-Elkayam
Production Controller John Casey
Jacket Designers Eleanor Bates, Sadie Thomas
Jacket Coordinator Elin Woosnam

First published in Great Britain in 2025 by Dorling Kindersley Limited
DK, 20 Vauxhall Bridge Rd, London SW1V 2SA

The authorised representative in the EEA is Dorling Kindersley Verlag GmbH. Arnulfstr. 124, 80636 Munich, Germany

Copyright © 2025 Dorling Kindersley Limited
A Penguin Random House Company
10 9 8 7 6 5 4 3 2 1
001–341092–Apr/2025

All rights reserved.
No part of this publication may be reproduced, stored in or introduced into a retrieval system, or transmitted, in any form, or by any means (electronic, mechanical, photocopying, recording, or otherwise), without the prior written permission of the copyright owner.

A CIP catalogue record for this book is available from the British Library.
ISBN: 978-0-2416-7565-6

Printed and bound in China

www.dk.com

This book was made with Forest Stewardship Council™ certified paper – one small step in DK's commitment to a sustainable future. Learn more at www.dk.com/uk/information/sustainability

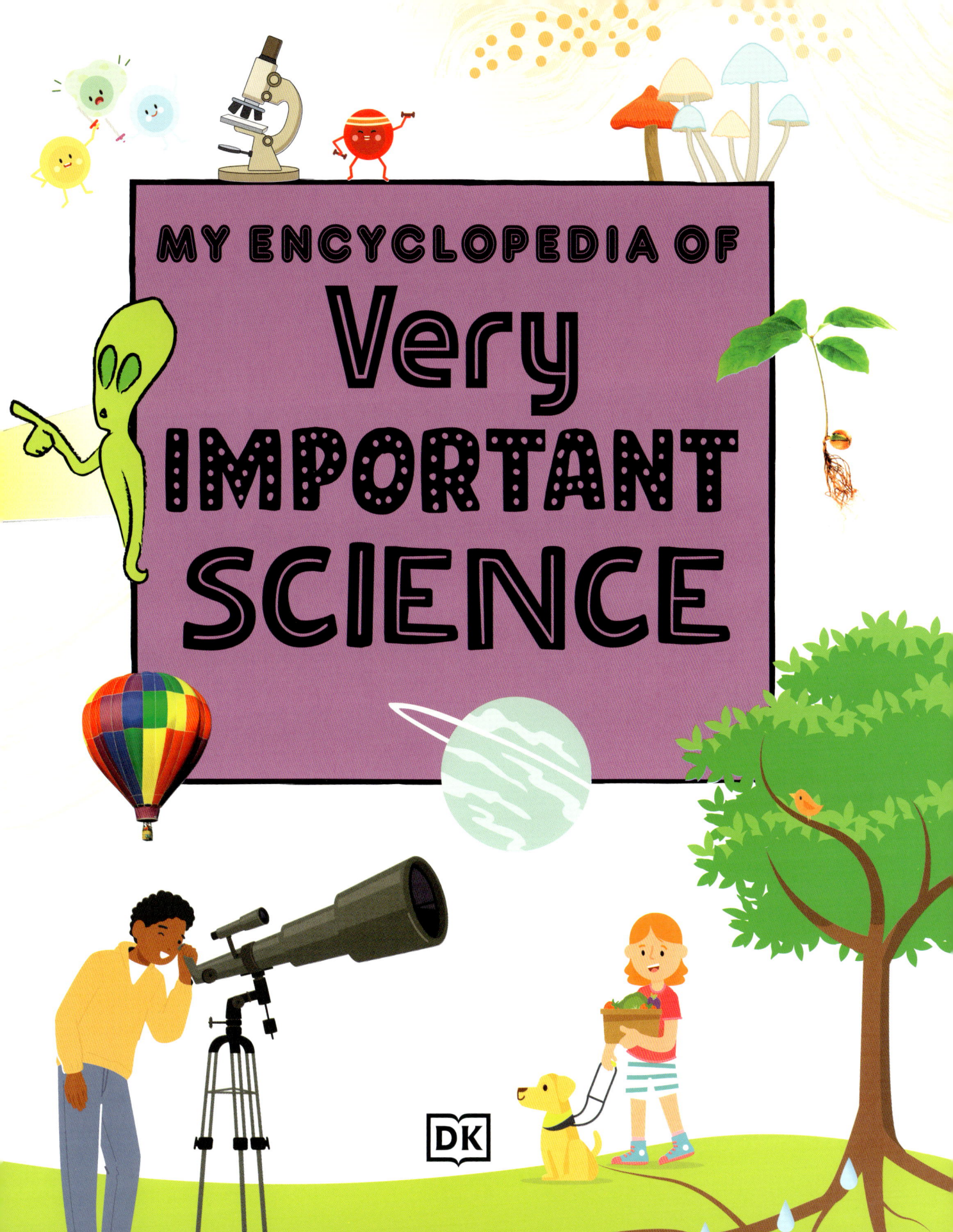

Contents

Matter

- 10 What is matter?
- 12 Tiny building blocks
- 14 Solids
- 16 Liquids
- 18 Gases
- 20 Changing state
- 22 Rocks and minerals
- 24 The rock cycle
- 26 Crystals
- 28 Elements
- 30 Mixtures
- 32 Compounds
- 34 Chemical reactions
- 36 Making fire
- 38 Acids and bases
- 40 What are metals?
- 42 Everyday metals
- 44 More metals
- 46 Nonmetals
- 48 Hydrogen, nitrogen, oxygen
- 50 Water
- 52 Carbon

Materials

- 56 What are materials?
- 58 Plastic fantastic
- 60 Glass
- 62 Ceramics
- 64 Synthetic fibres
- 66 Composites

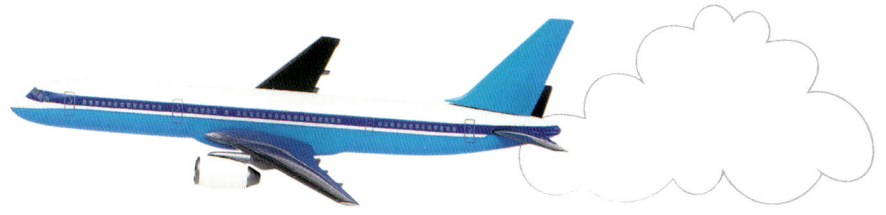

- 68 **Earth's resources**
- 70 **Factories at work**
- 72 **Recycling**
- 74 **Decomposers**

Forces

- 78 **What are forces?**
- 80 **The laws of motion**
- 82 **Turning forces**
- 84 **Friction**
- 86 **Gravity**
- 88 **S-t-r-e-t-c-h and... squash!**
- 90 **Simple machines**
- 92 **Engines**
- 94 **Flying high**
- 96 **Pressure**
- 98 **Floating and sinking**

Energy

- 102 **What is energy?**
- 104 **Types of energy**
- 106 **Energy on the move**
- 108 **Wave after wave**
- 110 **Heat**
- 112 **Hotter and colder**
- 114 **Nuclear energy**
- 116 **Changing energies**
- 118 **Sounds good**
- 120 **Light**
- 122 **Colour**
- 124 **Reflections**
- 126 **Refraction**
- 128 **A closer look**

Electricity and magnets

- 132 Electricity
- 134 Circuits
- 136 Static electricity
- 138 Magnets
- 140 Electromagnets
- 142 Using electricity
- 144 Supplying electricity
- 146 Energy sources
- 148 Electronics
- 150 Radio and television
- 152 Computers
- 154 The Internet
- 156 Robots

Space

- 160 The Universe
- 162 The Solar System
- 164 Rocky planets
- 166 Gas giants
- 168 Earth
- 170 The Moon
- 172 Space rocks
- 174 Twinkle, twinkle
- 176 Galaxies
- 178 Space travel

Life

- 182 What is life?
- 184 The kingdoms of life
- 186 Fossils

188 **Evolution**
190 **Microscopic life**
192 **Cells**
194 **Plants**
196 **Flowers and seeds**
198 **Soil**
200 **Fungi**
202 **What is an animal?**
204 **Animal groups**
206 **Metamorphosis**
208 **Habitats**
210 **Food chains**
212 **Endangered species**

214 **The human body**
216 **Nutrition**
218 **Science words**
220 **Index**
224 **Acknowledgements**

Matter

"Matter" is another word for **"stuff"**. That means **everything** – from the smallest speck of dust to the biggest structure on Earth – is made up of it. And yes, that includes every animal, plant, and even you!

What is matter?

Everything in the world and beyond is made of something. We call this something "**matter**", which is really a fancy way of saying "**stuff**". Different types of matter have different characteristics, which we call **properties**.

Floating and sinking

Some types of matter are **light**, and float on top of water. Others are **heavy** and sink to the bottom.

Bend or snap?

If you have ever tried to bend things, you will know that some of them can **bend without breaking**, and other things will **snap**. We call materials that are likely to snap **"brittle"**.

BEND   SNAP

There are a huge

Burning up

Most types of matter can be burned. However, some forms of matter completely **block heat** – it cannot travel through them at all. Materials that stop heat travelling are called **insulators**.

Electric flow

Electricity is able to flow through some materials, but not others. Materials that electricity can flow through are called **conductors**. We use them to control the flow of electricity.

Wood can be burned very easily.

Aerogel can block out most heat.

Hard and soft matter

We can look at how hard different minerals are by using a scale, called **Mohs scale**. It shows the **hardness** of 10 different minerals. Other minerals can then be compared against them.

Hardest

1 Talc
2 Gypsum
3 Calcite
4 Fluorite
5 Apatite
6 Feldspar
7 Quartz
8 Topaz
9 Corundum
10 Diamond

Softest

number of different types of matter.

Tiny building blocks

Everything in the world and beyond is made of something. We call these somethings **"matter"**, which is really a fancy way of saying **"stuff"**. Matter itself is made up of tiny little pieces, called particles.

Atoms
The tiny particles that everything is made of are called atoms. They are **extremely small** — so small that we can't see them.

Elements
An element is a thing that contains only **one type of atom**. There are 118 different elements altogether.

Gold
is made up of just gold atoms.

Coal
is made up of just carbon atoms.

Coal

Gold

There are atoms in the air, but they are more spaced out than atoms in liquids and solids.

Molecules

The atoms of some elements can **join together**, making groups of particles called molecules.

This picture shows atoms and molecules quite large. In reality, we can't even see them with a microscope.

For example, each **molecule of water** contains one oxygen atom and two hydrogen atoms.

Water molecule

You, your **clothes**, your **house**, your **school** — everything around you is made of atoms!

More than **7 billion** atoms can fit inside a full stop.

13

Solids

Just about everything you can think of exists in one of the **three states of matter – solid, liquid,** or **gas.** Solids have a clear shape, ranging from an aircraft to a zebra, and a lot of things in between.

Solid start
Look around you and you'll spot more solids than any other state of matter. They could be as stable as a **table**, as comfy as a **pillow**, as soft as **fur**, as bristly as a **hairbrush**, or as shiny as a **mirror**. But they are all solids.

Bonded together

Each state of matter is different because of the energy inside it. Energy is made of **tiny particles** that behave in different ways. The particles inside solids are **closely packed together**. They are held in place by powerful forces, known as bonds. This is why the particles stay in a fixed position, and solids keep their shape.

There is very little space between the particles.

Wooden brick

Solid stuff

You can **weigh** a solid and discover how heavy it is, and you can measure its **volume**. Some solids **break easily**, like glass, while others are strong, like metal. This depends on the strength of the bonds between the particles.

Metal cutlery

Diamond   Talc

Hard times

Minerals are solids that lie inside Earth's crust. Their **hardness** depends on how **strong** their bonds are. This is measured using the **Mohs scale**, with 10 being the hardest mineral (diamond) and 1 being the softest (talc).

Glass

Only about 30 per cent of your body is made of solid structures.

Liquids

Liquids are all around you, from the **juice** in your glass in the morning to the **water** running in your shower and the **blood** flowing through your veins.

Fill the space

Liquids don't keep the same shape. As their **particles rearrange** themselves, liquids **change** how they look. You can see this when you compare liquid that is stored inside a bottle to liquid poured into a glass. As a liquid **flows**, it adjusts to fill the shape of a container.

Room to roam

There is **more energy** inside liquids than solids. Particles inside liquids are not as tightly packed as in solids. Their **bonds are weaker**, so they can move around and slide past each other.

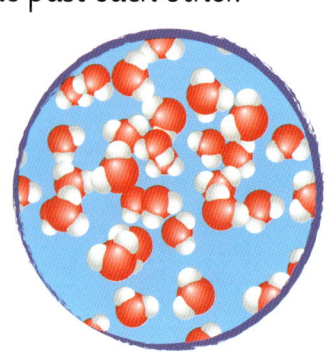

About 60 per cent of your body is liquid.

Liquid laws

You can learn about liquids in different ways. **Weighing** a liquid reveals how heavy it is. **Pouring** a liquid into a measuring jug shows its **volume**. Although a set amount of liquid can fill containers of different shapes, its volume **stays the same.**

Pancakes with maple syrup

Slow flow

Liquids flow at **different speeds**, and this is called their **viscosity**. Water has very **low** viscosity, so it flows **freely** and **easily**. When you cut your finger, **blood** seeps **slowly** because it has **high** viscosity. Maple syrup and honey can be slow to pour because they have even higher viscosity.

Honey

Nature in action

Liquids, particularly water, show their power in **nature**. Tidal waves can **wash away** coastlines, torrential rain can **pour** down from the skies, and rivers can **move water** from the land to the sea.

Strong waves

Rain caused by a typhoon

Gases

The third state of matter is gas. The air that surrounds us is full of **oxygen** and **nitrogen** gases, but as these are invisible, it's easy to forget we're breathing them in!

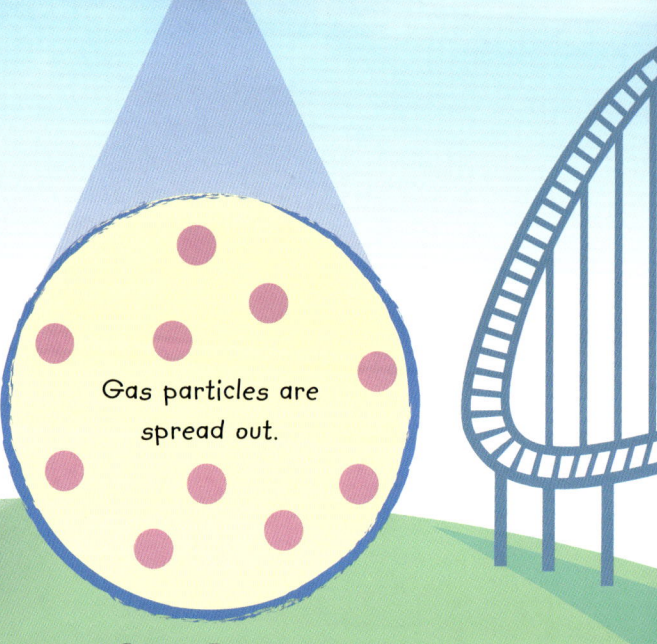

Gas particles are spread out.

On the loose
Particles inside gases have **more energy** than particles in solids and liquids, so they spread. Without any bonds, they have **large gaps** between them and whoosh around in all directions. No matter how big a space is, gases will spread out to fill it!

Gases inside a deodorant aerosol can escape from the nozzle.

Deodorant can

Understanding gases
It's hard to study gases when so many are **colourless** and can't be seen. They also **change shape** easily because of their fast particles. Gases in a container with no lid will escape into the air and spread out to fill a room, mixing with other gases. Despite this, scientists have found a way to weigh gases.

SPEEDY gas particles zip around at

It's a squeeze!

Unlike solids and liquids, gases can be **squashed** and **squeezed** to save space. This is called **compression**. Fizzy drinks contain **carbon dioxide** that has been dissolved into the drink. The gas **rushes** out when the bottle or can is opened. Compressed gas is also found inside fire extinguishers and safety features on roller-coasters.

Carbon dioxide escapes from a drink when the bottle is opened.

More matter

Most of the matter in the world is solid, liquid, or gas. But in space there is a fourth state of matter, called **plasma**. This special type of gas is found only at **sizzling hot** temperatures. Plasma exists inside **lightning**, the **Sun**, and all the **stars**.

Plasma gives off energy in the form of light.

more than 1,600 kph (1,000 mph)!

Iceberg

Changing state

Solids, liquids, and gases don't have to stay the same forever. They **transform** from one state of matter to another when their temperatures change.

Did you know?
Water is the only substance found naturally in all three states of matter – from solid icebergs to falling snowflakes, pouring rain to vast oceans, and sizzling hot springs to water vapour in the air.

Waterfall

When milk in a bottle freezes, the milk expands and pushes out through the top of the bottle.

Water ways
As water changes state, you can see it happen. At room temperature, water is **liquid**, and it runs and pours. When you turn on a tap, liquid water flows out.

Freezing
If the temperature of liquid water is lowered to 0°C (32°F) or below, water **freezes** and becomes **solid**. This solid form of water is ice. If you drop ice cubes into a drink the liquid cools down immediately.

Melting

When temperature rises above 0°C (32°F), water returns to its **liquid** form. If you leave an ice lolly out at room temperature, the ice **melts**. If you take your lolly outside in direct sunshine, the **heat** speeds up the process.

The Sun's rays melt the ice lolly back to liquid quickly.

If water vapour reaches colder air it condenses, forming a cloud of water droplets.

Evaporating

If you heat up water in a kettle, some of it will change from liquid to **gas**. As the water reaches **boiling point** at 100°C (212°F), liquid water **evaporates** into an invisible gas called **water vapour**.

Skipping a state

Most substances go through a liquid state to become a solid or gas. A few can **skip** from a **gas** to a **solid** and back again. When carbon dioxide gas freezes, it becomes a solid called dry ice, used on stages.

Carbon dioxide cools the air so clouds of liquid water droplets form.

Rocks and minerals

Earth's **outer layer** is made of solid rock. Rocks aren't the same all the way through – they are formed from a **mixture** of other substances, called minerals. Minerals cannot be broken down into smaller parts.

Rock types

1 **Sedimentary rock**
These rocks form when layers of **tiny pieces of mud or sand** get squashed together.

Limestone

Meteorites are rocks from space!

Multiple minerals

There are more than **4,000 different types** of minerals! They form in a range of places, including in rocks, in the sea, and deep inside Earth. Minerals can be found in rocks or exist by themselves.

Opal   Olivine

Amethyst

Rocks can form in **three** different ways:

2 **Igneous rock**
This forms when hot molten rock from under the Earth's **crust** comes to the surface through a crack or from a volcano, and cools down.

Gabbro

We can see the many minerals through a microscope.

3 **Metamorphic rock**
If an igneous or sedimentary rock is **squashed** or heated **inside Earth**, it becomes a metamorphic rock.

Marble

Some rocks glow in the dark!

A real gem
Some minerals can be cut and polished to create sparkling gems. Gems are often **worn as jewellery**, because they are beautiful to look at.

Uncut diamond

Cut diamond

23

The rock cycle

Rocks aren't quite as set in their ways as they look. Over millions of years they **form, move, melt, and get worn away**. We call this the rock cycle.

Liquid rock above Earth's surface is called lava. It is often thrown out as volcanoes erupt.

As the lava cools, it becomes solid igneous rock.

Liquid rock under Earth's surface is called magma. When magma cools, it can form areas of igneous rock.

Hot temperatures inside the Earth cause solid rocks to melt, becoming magma.

Land can be eroded (worn away),

Types of rock

There are **three** types of rock, and they all form **differently**:

Granite

Shale

Schist

Igneous
This rock forms when liquid rock cools and hardens. This can happen above or below the ground.

Sedimentary
This rock develops from layers of tiny pieces of rock, sand, or mud. As the layers build up, they get squashed, becoming rock.

Metamorphic
Sedimentary and igneous rock can change into metamorphic when a huge weight presses on the rock.

Wind and water wear away at rocks, making little bits of them break off.

Most of the stages in the rock cycle happen EXTREMELY SLOWLY.

Rivers carry along little pieces of rock, then drop them off in the sea.

Layers of sand or mud get slowly squashed together, forming sedimentary rock.

Deep underground, sedimentary rock can be heated and squeezed until it becomes metamorphic rock.

revealing the rocks underneath.

Crystals

Forming naturally in the Earth, crystals are solid substances made up of **regular** and **repeated patterns**. They can be as eye-catching as diamonds or as everyday as sugar and salt.

Rock solid
Crystals form when a liquid **cools down** and changes into a solid. When hot liquid magma from a volcano cools and **hardens** into rock, it can form crystals. The way crystals form is called crystallization.

A sugar crystal seen under a microscope.

Shaping up
Crystals have three-dimensional (3-D) structures with patterns that repeat. This makes crystals **stable and solid**. The shape of a crystal depends on how its atoms or molecules join together. Sugar crystal molecules lie in a column, while salt crystal molecules form a cube.

A salt crystal seen under a microscope.

Diamond is the world's HARDEST

Ruby
Diamond
Emerald

A snowflake seen under a microscope

Sparkle and shine

The most extraordinary crystals are precious stones that have been cut from rock and **polished**. Diamonds, rubies, and sapphires are crystals. Elements inside crystals give them their **beautiful colours**. For example, the metal element chromium makes emeralds green and rubies red.

Falling snow

Snowflakes are **ice crystals** that form inside rain clouds when the temperature drops and water freezes. Each one is unique, but they all have six sides or points because the molecules that make them up do, too.

Crystals help me move around, light up, and speak!

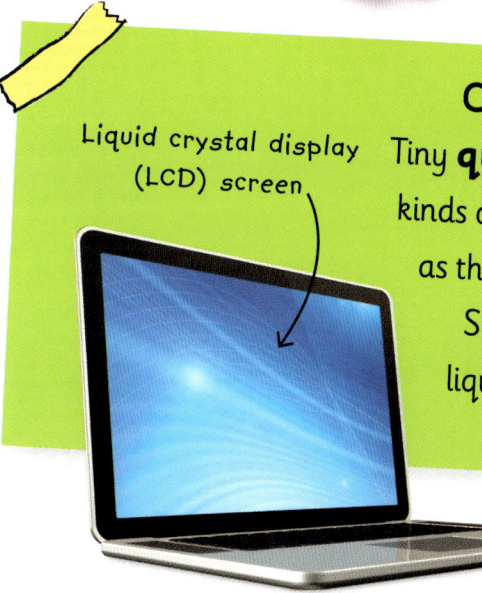

Liquid crystal display (LCD) screen

Clever crystals

Tiny **quartz crystals** are found in all kinds of things, from radios to watches, as they can create electrical signals. Some computer screens use liquid crystals in their displays.

Quartz sensors are used in robots.

substance and is very valuable!

Dmitri Mendeleev

In your element!

Did you know that your **entire body** is made of elements? More than 99 per cent of it is made from just **four** elements – nitrogen, hydrogen, carbon, and oxygen. There are even traces of gold inside you!

3% Other elements
3% Nitrogen
10% Hydrogen
19% Carbon
65% Oxygen

Organized elements

In 1869, Russian chemist **Dmitri Mendeleev** put together a **table** for the elements. He grouped together elements (with similar properties) in the same parts of the table, and left gaps for elements still to be discovered. This became known as the **periodic table**, and it's still used today.

Elements

Just about **everything** is made of elements. These simple substances **meet** and **mix** with each other to build the world around us.

Hydrogen is the MOST COMMON element in the Universe.

Chlorine

This element is a bright yellow gas at room temperature. Chlorine is such a powerful germ killer that it is often added to swimming pools to keep the water clean.

Everyday elements
There are **118 elements** in total, and **94** of them **exist naturally** in the world. Elements consist of one type of **atom**, and so they cannot be broken down any further.

Gold
Glittering gold is highly prized as a precious metal. Soft gold can be handcrafted into valuable jewellery, including necklaces, bracelets, and rings.

Sodium
Super-soft and bright white, sodium is a solid metal. You'll know sodium chloride as salt – we sprinkle it on our food to add flavour.

Sodium metal   Salt

Oxygen
This vital element keeps us alive. Oxygen is a colourless gas you can't see, but you inhale it to breathe.

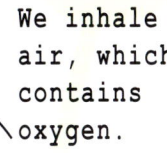

We inhale air, which contains oxygen.

Helium

A balloon filled with air drops to the ground because of air's density. If the balloon is filled with helium, it rises higher and higher because this gas is less dense than air.

Aluminium

This shiny, silver metal bends into all kinds of shapes, without actually breaking. Aluminium is handy for making drinks cans, kitchen foil, and bicycle frames.

Mixtures

You **make mixtures every day** without even realizing it. If you add water to fruit squash, sprinkle salt on food, or stir cake ingredients in a bowl, you've made a mixture!

Pieces of fruit in a yogurt are easy to spot.

Mixed up

Two or more different substances combine to make a mixture. Mixtures can be **solids, liquids, or gases**. Sometimes you can't see mixtures. For example, it's impossible to see the various gases that make up the air.

Types of mixture

There are three different types of mixtures – **solutions**, **suspensions**, and **colloids**.

Solutions are mixtures in which each part breaks down and mixes throughout. This can be seen when a drop of food colouring is added to water and transforms the whole colour.

This part of the water is cloudy as there are particles of flour in it.

Suspensions are mixtures in which solid pieces are spread out throughout the liquid. This can be seen in a muddy river or when we blend flour and water.

Colloids are mixtures in which the pieces are so small that they spread throughout and cannot be seen. A glass of milk or a pot of paint are both colloids.

Staying separate

Substances are **combined** in a mixture, but they are not **bonded**. This means no chemical reaction has taken place, so they can be separated again and returned to their individual substances.

Oil refineries use distillation to take petrol from crude oil.

Separating solids

Solids inside a liquid can be separated by **filtration** or **decantation**. Filtration involves tipping a liquid through a filter to leave behind solids, such as sand or salt. Decantation involves pouring out the liquid at the top, leaving the solid layer at the bottom. This process is used to get cream from milk.

Sand is suspended in water.

Sand remains in the filter.

Clean water is filtered out.

Separating liquids

Blended liquids are separated in a process called **distillation**. Firstly, the mixture is heated. When each liquid reaches its boiling point, it evaporates into a gas. When it has cooled, the gas returns to liquid and can be collected.

The ocean is the world's BIGGEST mixture! This mix of WATER AND SALT covers more than TWO-THIRDS of our planet.

Compounds

Compounds take mixtures to the next level! In a compound, **separate elements** are chemically **bonded** together to make something entirely different from their individual parts.

"Atom" comes from the Greek word for "indivisible". An atom cannot be broken down.

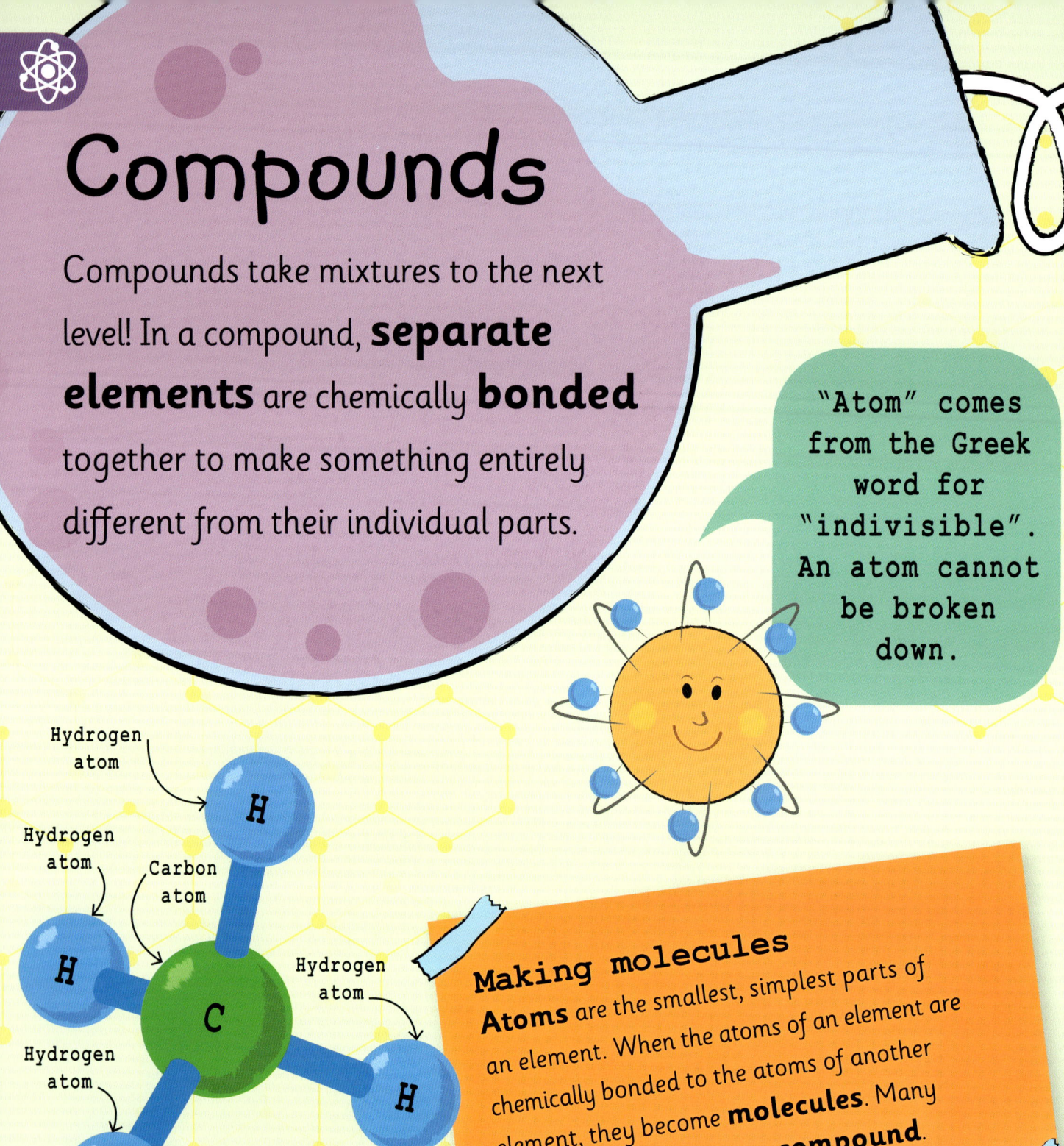

Methane molecule

Making molecules
Atoms are the smallest, simplest parts of an element. When the atoms of an element are chemically bonded to the atoms of another element, they become **molecules**. Many of these molecules make a **compound**.

Out of all the elements, HYDROGEN and

Total transformation

Compounds can **completely change** their elements to make something new. Sodium is a silvery metal, but when it combines with greenish chlorine gas, sodium chloride is made. This is better known as salt.

Sodium (Na) + Chlorine (Cl) = Sodium chloride (NaCl)

Back to basics

Taking a compound back to its original elements requires a lot of **heat** or **electricity**. A hot blast furnace is needed to separate out pure iron from iron oxide. An electrolyzer uses electricity to take apart the elements in water.

Common compound

Water is one of the most common compounds. It consists of two hydrogen atoms bonded to one oxygen atom to make a molecule of water. The chemical formula for water is H_2O.

Compounds are given chemical formulas to show the number of atoms.

CARBON make the most compounds.

Chemical reactions

A chemical reaction happens when one or more substances change to form a new one. These reactions range from fizzy, whizzy showstoppers that produce **bright light** and **heat** to changes that give no sign at all.

An apple a day
You may not notice chemical reactions happening. When you eat an apple, reactions inside your stomach help **digestion**. A chemical reaction with the air causes the leftover apple core to go **brown**. Another occurs when you wash your sticky hands!

Start to finish
The substances in a chemical reaction are called **reactants**. They may be a combination of atoms or compounds. They come together and **react** to each other to make a **product**.

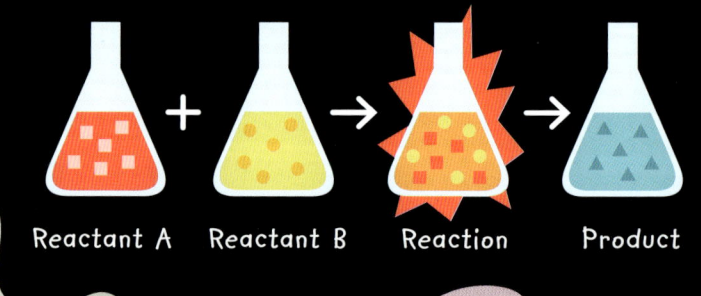

Reactant A   Reactant B   Reaction   Product

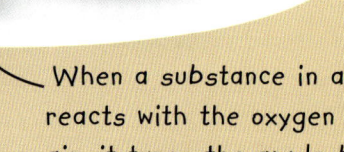

When a substance in apples reacts with the oxygen in the air, it turns the apple brown.

Reaction rate

A reaction can take place suddenly in the **blink of an eye**, like an explosion of dynamite, or it can take many weeks, like a tin can going rusty. The rate of the chemical reaction is known as the reaction rate. Mixing atoms together can make a reaction, but energy, such as electricity, heat, or sunshine, can **speed up** the reaction rate.

Compounds in dynamite react with oxygen to produce explosive heat and light.

Water and oxygen in the air start a chemical reaction that eventually turns a can rusty.

2 Hydrogen molecules ($2H_2$)   1 Oxygen molecule (O_2)   2 Water molecules ($2H_2O$)

Bond

Regroup and reform

Atoms are never **created** or **destroyed** during a reaction. The atoms react and break their bonds. They rearrange themselves into new molecules and form new bonds.

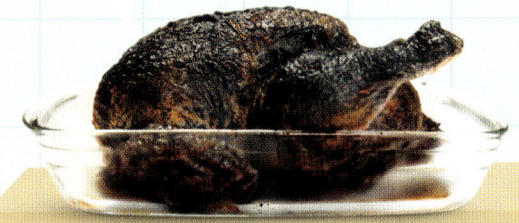

Permanent change

Many chemical reactions, such as burning, transform something totally, making it **impossible to return** it to its first form. If dinner is burnt, it becomes covered in charcoal and smoke. It can never turn back to its first form and a new meal will be on the menu!

A CHAIN REACTION describes a sequence of chemical reactions, such as burning fuel.

35

Making fire

There's nothing better than snuggling up by a **lovely warm fire** on a winter's night. But when the heat is on, what is really happening? Let's find out.

Fire away
Our ancient ancestors were lighting fires more than 500,000 years ago. This helped them to survive in **ice-cold habitats**. They used fire to **keep warm**, **cook meat**, and **scare away** animals.

Fire triangle
Three things are needed to start a fire and keep it burning: **fuel**, **oxygen**, and **heat**. If any one of these things is removed, the fire goes out.

Air is made up of about 20 per cent oxygen. Most fires need 16 per cent oxygen to burn. Oxygen is needed to keep the fire going.

A fire is started by applying a source of heat, such as a match to a fireplace. The heat must remain for the fire to keep burning.

The material used to make a fire is called the fuel. Wood is the most common but paper, plastics, and rubber are also fuels.

EARTH is the only planet with enough OXYGEN to make fire.

Combustion

During a fire, combustion occurs. This is when **burning fuel** reacts with oxygen to make **heat** and then **light**. The heat and light come in very handy for keeping warm and seeing in the dark, but fire must always be **handled with care**.

The hottest part of a flame or fire is near its base.

Fire extinguisher

Carbon dioxide

Putting it out

There are **three ways** to put out a fire. When the **fuel runs out**, the fire will stop. **Oxygen** can be removed by smothering the fire with carbon dioxide from a fire extinguisher. **Heat** can be removed by throwing water on the fire to cool it down.

Warning!
Fire is extremely dangerous. It spreads quickly, and it easily gets out of control. Never play with matches or get too close to a fire.

Acids and bases

Oranges and lemons are full of **tangy** acid, while green vegetables have the **bitter** flavour of bases. Some acids and bases can kill bugs, dissolve metals, or clean drains!

Limes are more acidic than lemons.

Fruity feast

Acids are chemical substances that are common in different foods. Many fruits – including oranges and limes – contain **citric acid**, which creates a strong, sour sensation in the mouth.

Lemon juice is acidic enough to **WEAR AWAY**

Helpful acid

Your tummy is home to some seriously strong acid that, outside of the body, can burn materials! **Hydrochloric acid** helps break down the food you've eaten. It also protects you by wiping out bad bugs that could otherwise make you ill.

Neutral ground

What do you get if you **mix an acid with a base**? They cancel each other out! They are no longer an acid or a base, but somewhere between the two. This is known as neutral. Water is a neutral substance.

Coming clean

The opposite of an acid is called a **base**. Bases are often found in **cleaning products**, including bleach, soap, and toothpaste. They are tough on fats, oils, and dirt. Bases are also used in **medicines** to keep the body healthy.

Soap is good for cleaning skin.

After eating acidic foods, help protect your teeth by drinking lots of water before you brush them.

the hard white enamel covering your teeth.

Rain risk

Chemicals such as sulphuric acid can get into the air and mix with water that then falls as acid rain. **Acid rain** can kill plants and wear away buildings.

WARNING!

Beware of the strongest acids and bases, such as cleaning products. They are dangerous, and should never be touched or tasted.

What are metals?

Most metals are **strong**, and can be bent and **moulded** to make different things. They are **shiny**, and are usually solid at room temperature.

Uses of metals

Most metals are **good conductors**, which means heat and electricity can pass through them. This makes them very useful.

Cooking pot

Copper wire

In the mix

Combining different metals together can make a mix that has **features of both types**. Mixing tin and copper makes bronze, which is much stronger than either metal it is made from.

Bronze bell

Bronze reacts with oxygen in the air. This oxidization makes the metal turn green.

Copper can kill bacteria and viruses.

Copper kettle

Rhodium

Rhodium is a RARE METAL that is 10 times more valuable than gold!

Horseshoe

Metals can be made into different shapes. We heat them up and bend them into new shapes, or melt them down and pour them into moulds. Once the metal cools down again, it keeps its new shape.

Mining metal

Metals are found in rocks called ores. To get the metal out and be able to use it we have to dig the rocks out of the ground and then heat them up.

The ores are dug out of the ground in places called mines.

The ore is broken up and heated, to remove the metal.

The metal cools down and becomes solid. It can now be used.

Everyday metals

We see metals in use around us every day! Different metals have different **properties**, or features, so they are used for different things.

Electric!
Copper is a metal that is **fairly soft** and easy to shape. It is also good at carrying electricity. So, we use it to make electrical wires.

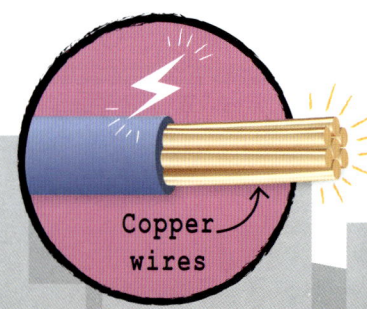
Copper wires

Steel is a good metal for making skyscrapers.

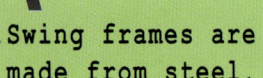
Swing frames are made from steel.

Light and strong
Titanium is a metal that is very **light**, but also extremely **strong**. It is often used to make bicycle frames.

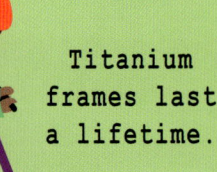
Titanium frames last a lifetime.

Use and reuse
Aluminium is light, can be easily shaped, and **doesn't rust**. It can also be recycled, which means it is perfect for making drinks cans.

Iron is the MOST COMMON

Shiny and bright
Gold is a metal that is **easily shaped**. It also has a beautiful yellow colour, too, so we like making jewellery out of it.

Planes are made mainly out of aluminium.

Strong as steel
Mixing **iron** with a bit of **carbon** makes a new metal called steel. Steel is stronger than pure metal, which makes it useful for large building projects.

Super steel
This is one of the most common and most often used metals. We use it to make **all sorts of things**, including cars, ships, and buildings.

metal in the WHOLE Universe.

More metals

There are so many **types of metals** that you are not likely to have heard of all of them. Here are some of the **less usual** types.

A roll of lead roofing

Poor metals
This group of metals are soft and **melt easily**. Lead is a poor metal. It was once used to make roofs and pipes. However, we now know it is poisonous, so it is not used much any more.

Alkali metals
This group of metals react quickly with other things. They are shiny, and soft enough to be **easily sliced** with just a knife. Sodium is an alkali metal. We eat it every day, in the form of sodium chloride – salt.

Until the 1900s, lead was commonly used in oil paint.

OIL PAINT

Arsenic is a metalloid.

Alkaline earth metals

These metals are soft and shiny. Each of them produces a **bright colour** when burned, which makes them useful for colouring fireworks.

Barium burns green

Calcium burns orange

Magnesium burns bright white

Strontium burns red

Metalloids

The metalloids act like both metals and nonmetals. For example, they are semiconductors. This means that **electricity can move through them**, but not very easily.

Silicon is a metalloid that is used to make computer microchips.

It is also EXTREMELY poisonous!

Nonmetals

Everything on Earth is formed from **elements** – things that cannot be split into smaller parts. Almost all of the elements are types of metals. Some are not metal, so we call them nonmetals.

Helium is very light. We use it to make balloons float upwards.

Noble gases

Gases in this group don't have colour, smell, or taste – they are **hard to spot**! They usually stay as they are, without interacting with other elements. There are seven noble gases, including helium, argon, and neon.

Argon doesn't let heat move through it, so we use it to keep things warm or cool. For example, we put argon gas between layers of glass in windows to insulate our homes.

Neon shines brightly when electricity flows through it. We use it to make glowing signs.

There are 17 NONMETAL elements.

Halogens

These elements **react quickly with other elements**. Fluorine, chlorine, bromine, iodine, and astatine are halogens.

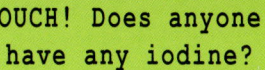

OUCH! Does anyone have any iodine?

We use **chlorine** to kill germs in our swimming pools.

Iodine is used to clean wounds.

Carbon

All life on Earth is made from carbon: plants, animals, and humans. Diamonds and coal are also formed from carbon.

Sulphur

This nonmetal is bright yellow! It is found as crystals near volcanoes and hot springs. Sulphur has an **unusual smell**, a little like rotten eggs.

YUK! That stinks!

Sulphur comes out of volcanoes as gas or molten rock.

47

Nitrogen, oxygen, and hydrogen

The air around us is made of a mixture of things called **gases**. We can't see them, but they are definitely there! Two of the main gases in air are **nitrogen** and **oxygen**.

21% OXYGEN

1% other stuff

78% NITROGEN

Up in the air

The **main gases** in the air are nitrogen and oxygen. There are also smaller amounts of lots of other gases, including hydrogen and carbon dioxide.

Gases are invisible in the air but they can be seen in bubbles.

Nitrogen, oxygen, and

Nitrogen

As a gas, nitrogen makes up **most of our air**. As a liquid, it is extremely cold and can be used to cool things down fast. Nitrogen in compounds is used to help crops grow.

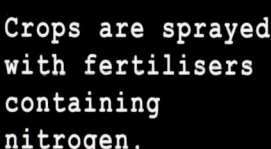

Crops are sprayed with fertilisers containing nitrogen.

Oxygen

Most types of life on Earth need to **breathe in oxygen** to stay alive. Animals do this with special organs called gills and lungs.

A horse's lungs can hold 10 times as much air as a human's.

Hydrogen

This is the **lightest thing** on Earth! It is also very easy to burn. Hydrogen fuel has been used to help launch rockets into space.

Rockets use liquid hydrogen to blast off.

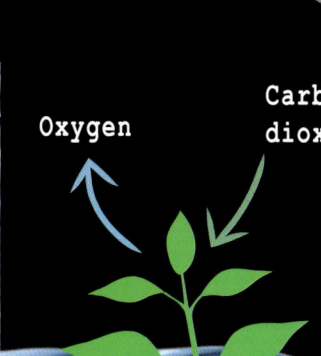

Oxygen   Carbon dioxide

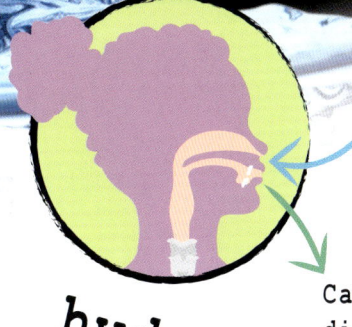

Oxygen

Carbon dioxide

In and out

Animals breathe in **oxygen** and breathe out **carbon dioxide**. Plants take in carbon dioxide and send out oxygen.

hydrogen are all gases with NO COLOUR.

Water

Water is very important for keeping us and everything else on Earth **alive**!

Solid　　　　Liquid　　　　Gas

Liquid, solid, gas
Water is a **liquid**. However, when it gets very cold it freezes, becoming **solid ice**. When it gets very hot, it becomes a gas called **water vapour**.

71 per cent of Earth's surface is covered in water.

Precious liquid
Humans, animals, and plants all need water to live. Earth is the only place in space that we know has **liquid water** on its surface. It is also the only place that we know has **living things**. Without water, we would not exist!

The water cycle

Water is always moving. This process is called the water cycle. It has four main stages.

Water vapour in the air groups together as clouds.

Rain, snow, and hail fall from the clouds onto land.

Rivers carry water into the sea.

Water vapour from the sea travels into the air.

Water at home

We need water every day — as well as drinking it, we use water for washing, cleaning, cooking, and even to heat our homes. To carry so much water around we have **networks of pipes**, which bring clean water to us and take dirty water away.

From rivers to oceans

Water can be found all over Earth. It fills our oceans and lakes, and flows across the land as rivers and streams. Water **shapes the land** as it moves, steadily wearing rocks down and carrying the pieces away.

Carbon

Carbon is **an element** – a substance that can't be broken down to make other things. It can come in a range of different forms.

From coal to diamonds

Like all elements, carbon is **made up of atoms**. Carbon is unusual because its atoms can be arranged in many ways, making different things.

Coal Diamond

Graphite

Carbon is in the **air we breathe** – it forms a gas called carbon dioxide. Every time you breathe out, you send out carbon dioxide that your body doesn't need.

Living carbon

All living things contain carbon, too. That includes plants, animals, and you! Around **one-fifth** of your body is made up of carbon.

Plants

Animals

Humans

Carbon forms more than 10 MILLION different substances.

Fossil fuels

Over millions of years, dead plants and animals get squashed together until the carbon inside them changes and they form **oil**, **gas**, and **coal**. We call these "fossil fuels".

Oil is mined from the ground and used to make electricity.

On the move

Carbon doesn't stay trapped in one form. It can move between solid, liquid, and gas. This process is called the **carbon cycle**.

Plants take in lots of carbon dioxide, and give out some oxygen

Carbon dioxide gas is in the air

Animals (including humans) breathe out carbon dioxide

Oceans take in and release carbon dioxide

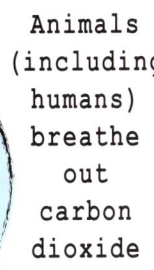

Factories let out carbon dioxide

Animals take in carbon dioxide by eating plants

Animals release carbon when they poo

Fossil fuels are under the oceean

Dead plants and animals rot away or slowly turn into fossil fuels

Fossil fuels release carbon dioxide when they are burned

Materials

What things are made of matters. Imagine if kettles were made of chocolate and helmets were made of glass – they would not be very good at their jobs! This chapter is all about **how we make**, **use**, and **reuse materials** every single day.

What are materials?

Everything around us is made of something. In science, these things are known as materials. Some are **natural**. Others are made by people **mixing** natural things together, or by scientists in laboratories.

Nylon and polyester are created in a lab and used to make clothing.

Natural materials

Some materials come from plants or animals, or are dug up from the ground. Here are a few examples:

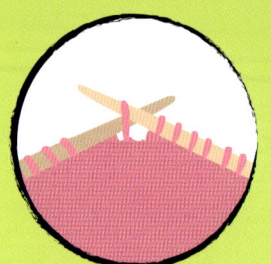

Wool is fur, usually from sheep. It can be woven or knitted to make warm clothes.

Rubber is the sap of a rubber tree. We use it to make rubber bands as it is stretchy.

Wood comes from trees. We build things with it, and also burn it to make heat.

Stone is found on and under the ground. We use it for buildings.

Metal is dug up from the ground. It is hard and strong, and can be shaped easily.

Materials made by humans

Drinking glasses

Checked fabric

Glass
We make glass by **heating up sand** until it melts. Glass is see-through and hard, which makes it useful for making things such as drinking glasses.

Fabric
Fabric is made by weaving **lots of little threads** together. The threads can come from natural materials, such as wool, or be artificially made, usually from plastic.

Plastic bottle

Plastic
Plastic is **waterproof** and **light**, and comes in a range of different types. We use it to make all sorts of things, from bottles to toys.

Ceramics
Ceramics are produced by **baking clay** in a very hot oven. They are hard, but can be easily broken.

Ceramic pot

Composite materials
Mixing different materials together can create new materials that have the **best features** of both materials. They are called composites.

Bike frames are often made of a composite called carbon fibre.

Plastic

Strands of carbon

Carbon fibre is made of tiny strands of carbon in plastic. It is very strong but also light.

Plastic fantastic

Plastic is a material that is **strong**, waterproof, cheap to make, **easy to shape**, hard to break, and doesn't let electricity pass through it. This makes plastic very useful, and we create and use huge amounts of it.

Shaping plastic

Most plastic is shaped by being **heated up** and then **poured into moulds** to set. The plastic then takes on the shape of the moulds.

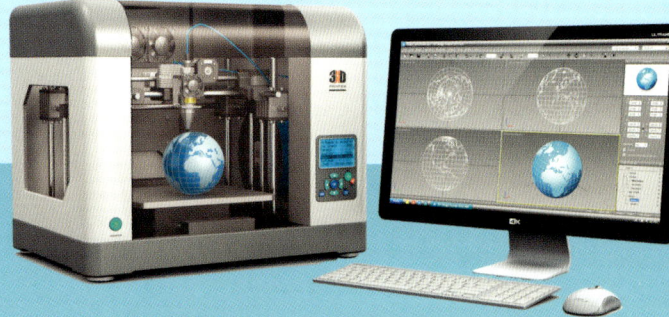

3-D printers print using layers of plastic. They can create almost any shape.

Making plastic

Most types of plastic are **synthetic** and made from oil, which is pumped up from deep underground. Some plastics can be **found naturally** in plants, insects, milk, and animal horns.

Plastics made from plant material are called bioplastics.

Hanging around

Plastic lasts for a very long time. This is good when we're using it, but **bad for the environment**. All the plastic we have ever made still exists, and will not rot away completely for hundreds of years.

Plastic rubbish can harm wildlife.

The first synthetic plastic was invented in the 1850s.

Plastic was used to help save trees! In 1959, Swedish engineer Sten Gustaf Thulin invented plastic bags, as an alternative to paper bags.

New life

Some types of plastic can be turned into new things, in a process called recycling. For example, plastic bottles can be recycled to make **seatbelts, carpets, and clothes**.

Glass

See-through and **easy to shape**, glass is a very useful material. To make it, sand is mixed with other chemicals and then heated up until the **sand and chemicals** melt together.

Glass-blowing is an ancient form of art.

Taking shape

For thousands of years, people have **shaped glass** by blowing into it when it is hot and liquid. This process is called **glass-blowing**.

Before plastic was invented, glass

Breakable
Glass cannot be bent. It is **fragile**, and can shatter into pieces. Smashed glass is sharp and can hurt you.

Safety glass
Glass can be **layered with plastic** to create a strong, see-through material that sticks together if it smashes. Car windscreens are made of this "safety glass".

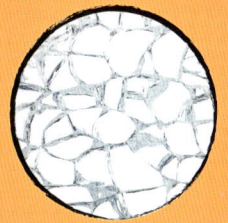
Safety glass

Normal glass

Modern glass
These days, glass is usually **made in a factory**. Machines can make glass objects much more quickly than people can, while making sure that all the objects are identical.

See-through art
Glass comes in all sorts of different **colours**, and can be beautiful to look at. Some artists specialize in glass, and it has been used in the **windows** of religious buildings for centuries.

was the only SEE-THROUGH material.

Ceramics

Some types of **clay** become solid and **very hard** if they are baked. We call them ceramics. You probably know ceramics from the **cups, plates,** and **bowls** you use every day, but they have plenty of other uses, too.

Works of art

Artists have shaped and coloured ceramics for thousands of years. Colours can be **painted** on before the clay is fired in a special oven, called a **kiln**. The colours become brighter in the kiln.

Making ceramics

To turn clay **hard**, it must be baked at an extremely **high temperature**. This is called **firing**.

1 Shaping clay

The clay is **moulded** into the desired shape while it is wet.

Blocking electricity

Ceramic materials are **insulators**, which means electricity cannot flow through them. They are used in machines to **control the flow** of electricity, protecting us from dangerous electric shocks.

Ceramic is used in a car's spark plug

Ceramic tiles on a space shuttle

Blastoff!

Some ceramics withstand very **high temperatures** without being damaged. **A spacecraft** can be covered in layers of ceramic tiles, to protect it from extreme heat in space.

Ceramics are hard but also brittle. They are stiff, not flexible, and will break into pieces if smashed.

Useful material

Ceramics don't react with water or other materials. This means they are safe to use **inside our bodies**, to make new joints and **false teeth**.

Ceramics can be formed into almost any shape. They can't be burned and are shiny and easy to clean. This makes them useful for all sorts of things, such as bathroom fittings and plates.

2 Firing

The moulded object is put into a **kiln** to be fired.

3 Completed

Once fired, the **hard item** will not change shape.

Synthetic fibres

A fibre is a thin thread. Fibres can be twisted together to make rope, or woven to make cloth. Humans have **invented new fibres** that allow us to make cloth with properties that natural fibres don't have.

Natural fibres

Some types of fibre occur naturally, in animals or plants. They include **wool**, **cotton**, and **silk**. Humans have been using these fibres for thousands of years!

Wool is fur, usually from a sheep.

Cotton comes from the fluffy white seeds of a cotton plant.

Silk comes from the cocoon of a particular type of moth.

Inventing materials

New fibre can be made by **mixing lots of chemicals** together. Once mixed, the liquid is pushed through tiny holes that shape it into strings.

Machines can make large quantities of fibres.

Microfibres

Some synthetic fibres are smaller than natural ones. Microfibres are many times **thinner than human hairs**. They can be used to make cloths that take in a lot of water and pick up dust – perfect for cleaning.

Useful fibres

Here are a few examples of fibres humans have invented, and what makes them useful.

Rayon is smooth, soft, and waterproof.

Nylon is very strong.

Spandex is smooth and stretchy.

Acrylic is warm, strong, and light.

Polyester is strong and hard to wear out.

Rotting away

Many synthetic fibres **contain plastic**. This means that it will take them longer to rot away than natural fibres. Your outgrown clothes could take up to 200 years to rot away!

Used clothes at a landfill site.

65

Composites

Composites are materials that are made from **two or more things** that have been mixed together. Composites aim to take the best features of each material, and combine them into something even better.

Concrete and steel can resist damage and last a long time.

Building high
Many of our buildings are made of a mixture of **concrete and steel**. The steel structure strengthens the concrete, letting us build taller buildings than we could with just concrete.

"Composite" means "made up of several parts".

Mud bricks
Mud and straw can be mixed together to make strong mud bricks. They have been used for thousands of years and are still made today!

Liftoff!

Space travel uses lots of complicated parts. Scientists use high-tech composites to help them make spacecraft that are **light and strong**.

A rocket's body is often made from a carbon fibre composite.

Superstrong

Kevlar is a material that is stronger than steel, heat-resistant, and almost **impossible to stretch**. It is used in tyres, aircraft, and protective clothing.

We have been making composites for thousands of years!

Fibreglass kayaks are light and stiff, which means it can glide through water.

Fibreglass

This material is made from **plastic and glass**. It is less likely to smash than glass, and can be shaped in all sorts of ways, making it super useful.

Earth's resources

Our planet is home to all sorts of useful things, which we **eat, build with, burn**, and so on. We call these things resources.

Wood
We use wood from trees to build things, to **make paper**, and to burn. People plant new forests, but many of them have already been cut down.

Gathering logged trees

Coal takes 300 million years to form.

Fossil fuels
Oil, coal, and gas are known as fossil fuels. We burn them to **make energy**. However, these resources cannot be replaced. One day, we will have used them up.

Digging up coal

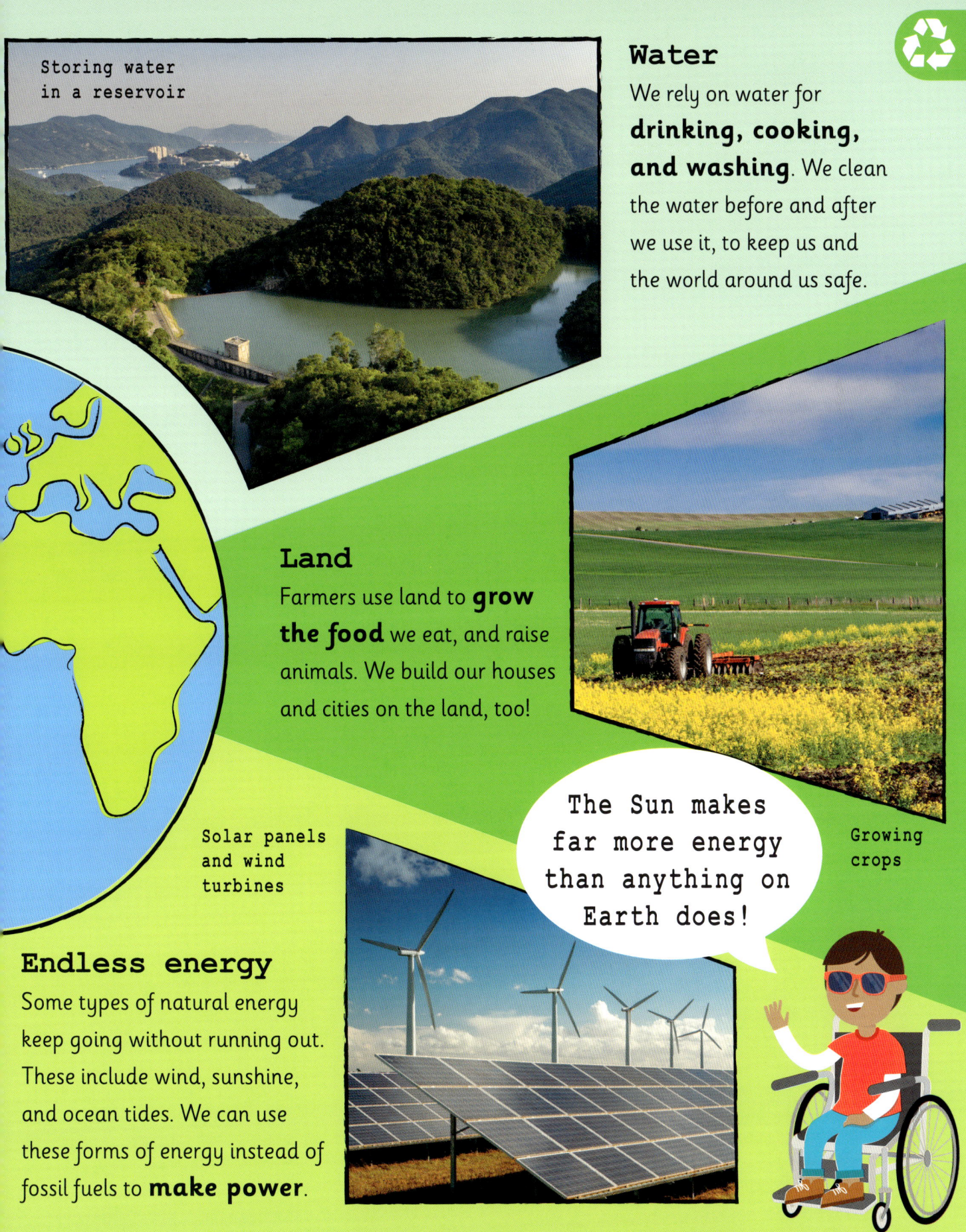

Storing water in a reservoir

Water
We rely on water for **drinking, cooking, and washing**. We clean the water before and after we use it, to keep us and the world around us safe.

Land
Farmers use land to **grow the food** we eat, and raise animals. We build our houses and cities on the land, too!

Growing crops

Solar panels and wind turbines

The Sun makes far more energy than anything on Earth does!

Endless energy
Some types of natural energy keep going without running out. These include wind, sunshine, and ocean tides. We can use these forms of energy instead of fossil fuels to **make power**.

1 **Raw materials**
These are the things that are **used to make** the product.

2 **Simple stages**
A complicated process is broken down into **smaller chunks**. A chain of tasks is called an **assembly line**.

The best fabric is chosen for the item of clothing.

Fabric is cut, ready for sewing.

Factories at work

Factories make all kinds of things, such as food, furniture, and cars. This one is making clothes.

Factories are places where **things are made**. Good factories can make things quickly, cheaply, and always very well.

Robots
Some tasks are difficult or dangerous for humans, so factories have robots that do these jobs instead. Robots can do **easy, repetitive jobs** too, to save humans time.

A robot making cars

"Each piece of the garment is sewn by a different person."

"Machines help people work quickly and accurately."

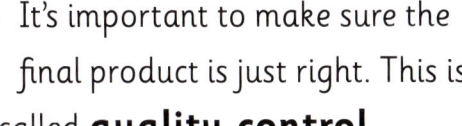

3 Final check

It's important to make sure the final product is just right. This is called **quality control**.

Rejected clothes

A robot lifting bottles of water

Before factories

Factories became common during the **Industrial Revolution**, a time of great change around 200 years ago. Before that, people made things by hand. This was slow and expensive, which meant that not much stuff could be made. Factories were often unsafe places for people to work in.

Recycling

When we make **something new** out of rubbish, we are recycling it, rather than burning it or burying it underground. Recycling things means there is less need to make new stuff, which is better for our planet.

What can be recycled?
Not everything can be recycled. Some of the **materials** that are **most often** recycled are paper, metal, plastic, and cardboard.

Paper

Metal

Plastic

Cardboard

Not all TYPES OF PLASTIC can be recycled yet.

How is it done?

Different materials are recycled differently. Usually the used items are **sorted** and cut up into little pieces. Then the pieces are **melted** down and chopped into pellets so they can be **moulded**. Here's how it works for plastic:

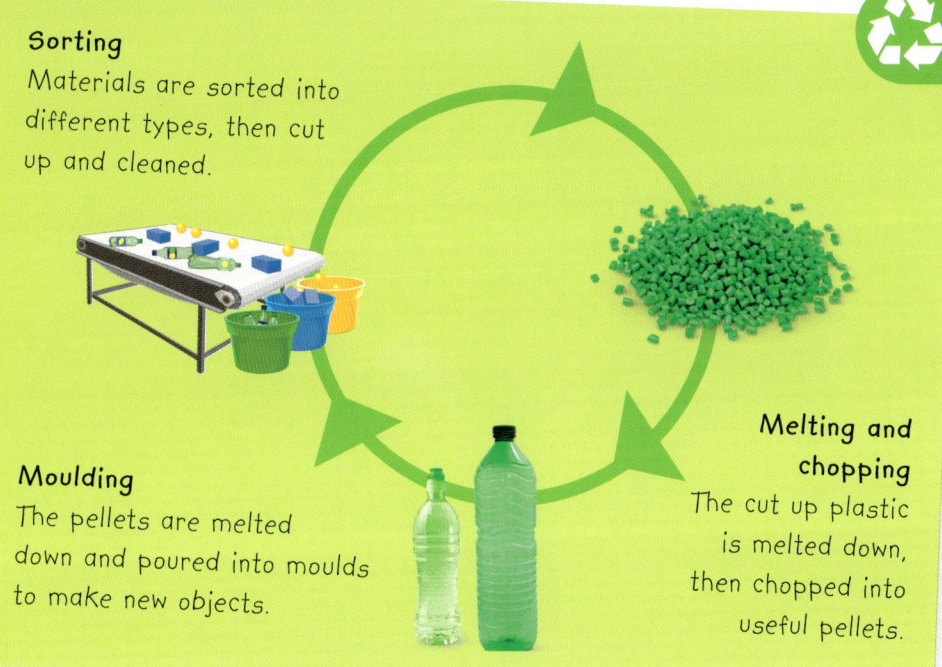

Sorting
Materials are sorted into different types, then cut up and cleaned.

Moulding
The pellets are melted down and poured into moulds to make new objects.

Melting and chopping
The cut up plastic is melted down, then chopped into useful pellets.

Reusing

Recycling saves waste, but it still takes a lot of energy and effort. It is even **better for our planet** if we can reuse what we already have, without making it into something new.

Landfill

Much of the rubbish that we **cannot recycle** is sent to landfill. We bury it in huge pits in the ground. This is bad for the land and animals around it, and the waste takes ages to rot away.

Upcycling

Taking something you no longer use and **making** it into **something new** is called upcycling. Upcycling is another way of avoiding waste. Here are a few ideas:

Make a bag from old jeans.

Turn tin cans into plant pots.

Paint an old chest of drawers in bright colours or patterns.

Decomposers

Decomposers are Earth's clean-up crew, and the best recyclers. They break down **dead plants** and **animals** and recycle the best bits.

Toadstool

Bacteria

Bacteria and protozoa
These tiny living things are **so small** we can only see them with a microscope.

Meet the decomposers

Fungi
Fungi, such as toadstools, use special substances called **enzymes** to get food from dead things.

Detritivores
These animals, which include earthworms, survive by **gobbling up waste**.

Earthworm

How decomposers work

1 Animals and plants die. They are made of complicated structures, such as skin, muscle, leaves, and bark.

2 Decomposers get to work! They start eating up the remains.

3 From the dead matter, decomposers can get the energy they need to grow and reproduce.

4 What comes out of decomposers is much simpler than what goes in. They leave behind substances such as water, carbon dioxide, and nutrients.

5 These simple substances are exactly what plants and animals need to grow.

Decomposers recycle energy in nature.

Forces

Forces can seem like magic! They work invisibly to **move**, **shape**, and **change** objects all around us. But they are all created and controlled by the **rules of science**, which tell us exactly how they work.

What are forces?

Forces are **pushes** or **pulls** that make things happen. Some of these pushes and pulls are **created by us**. Others happen without us doing anything.

Pushing force

Making movement

Forces can make things **move** or **stop** moving. They can change the speed of movement, making it **faster or slower**. Forces can also make a moving object spin.

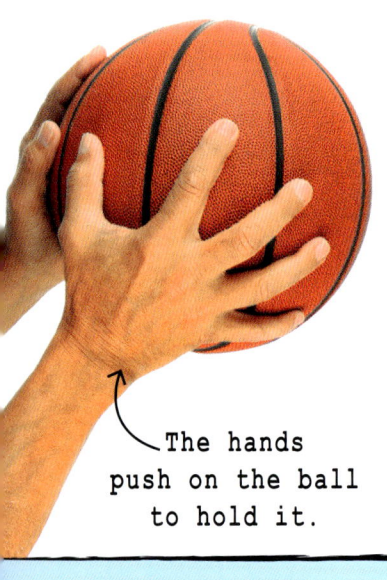

The hands push on the ball to hold it.

I mustn't lose my grip!

Balanced forces

Balanced forces

Objects can be pushed and pulled by **different forces** at the same time. If the forces acting on something are balanced, the object will be still, or move along at a steady pace. If one force is bigger than the other, the object will speed up or slow down.

1 Both teams are pulling equally hard. The forces are balanced, so there is no movement.

Pushing forces

A push can make things **start moving** or make them faster if they are already moving. It is a movement away from the place the pushing motion comes from.

Pulling forces

A pull can also make things start moving or move them faster. It is a movement towards the place the **pulling motion** comes from.

are OPPOSITE in direction BUT EQUAL in size.

2 The team on the left is pulling harder, creating a pulling force towards it.

3 The team on the right is pulling harder, creating a pulling force towards it.

The laws of motion

When things move, they usually move in certain types of ways. In the 17th century, an English scientist called Isaac Newton wrote descriptions of **three ways things move**. He called them the "laws of motion", and they happen all around us.

Kicking a ball

1st law — Staying still

The first law is that objects stay still **unless** they are **pushed or pulled**. For example, a ball stays still on the ground until it is kicked.

I wrote a book about the three laws in 1686.

Isaac Newton

The swing stays still until it is pushed.

All movements and actions involve FORCES.

2nd law — How fast?

The second law is that the amount an object speeds up depends on two things: **how heavy the object is**, and **how big the force is that pushes or pulls it**. The harder an object is hit, the faster it will move, and the further it will travel.

The harder the baseball is hit, the further it will go.

A child's force is less than a grown-up's.

3rd law — Matching forces

The third law is that there are always **two forces** working on an object, in opposite directions. So, when one force **acts** on an object, its opposite force **reacts** against it.

Action: The rocket blasts out burning gas at high speed.
Reaction: The rocket is pushed upwards away from the gas.

Every action has an equal and opposite reaction.

Action: The ball hits the ground.
Reaction: The ground pushes the ball upwards.

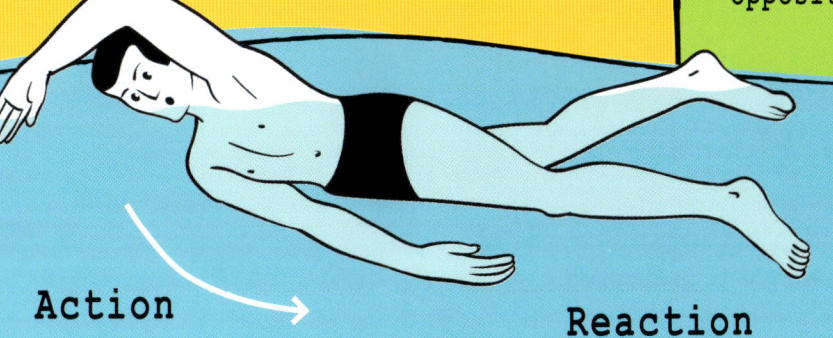

Action: The swimmer pushes water backwards away from them.
Reaction: The water pushes the swimmer forwards.

Action →   ← Reaction

Turning forces

If moving things are left alone, they move in straight lines. To **move in circles**, they need turning forces. Turning forces can make moving objects **spin, twist, and twirl around**.

Gears turn around

Circling around
One force makes things move in circles around a **central point**. This is called **centripetal force**, because centripetal means "centre-seeking".

The hammer weighs about the same as a bowling ball!

Hammer thrower

Centripetal force

Hammer spins around

Central point

Spinning a ball on a rope creates a circular force.

Spinning along
Gears are circles with teeth around the edges, which allow a turning force **to be passed along**. As one gear turns, its **teeth turn** the **next gear**, and so on.

Hurricane with spinning winds

Circular storm
A hurricane is a huge storm. Air is **pulled into its centre** at **top speeds**, making the whole hurricane spin as it moves along.

The BIGGER a force, the MORE IT CAN TURN something.

Pivots
Forces can turn around **fixed points**, called pivots. Seesaws work this way: the straight part of the seesaw that you sit on moves up and down across a fixed point.

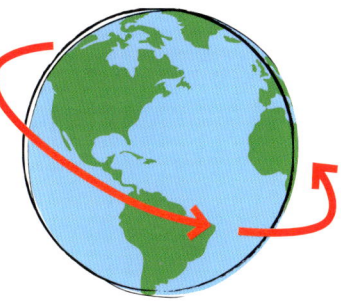

Our planet is constantly spinning, but we can't feel it.

The fixed point in the middle of the seesaw is the pivot.

The path of the seesaw is slightly curved.

Friction

Friction is a **force** that acts in the opposite direction to the movement of an object, **slowing the object down**. The surfaces of moving objects create friction as they move past each other.

How much friction?

Rough surfaces create more friction than smooth surfaces. **Rough** surfaces have more **grip**, whilst **smooth** surfaces, such as ice, are **slippery**.

Ice-skates have very smooth edges on the bottom. These don't create much friction, so you can easily slide along ice.

Walking boots have rough soles with thick ridges on them. These create lots of friction and grip onto the ice.

Warming up

Friction produces heat. When you **rub your hands** together, there is friction between their surfaces. Heat is produced, and your hands start to get warm.

Wearing away

Friction can **rub at things** over time, wearing them away. This can be annoying – it might mean that rubbed away parts need to be replaced. However, it is sometimes useful – for example, we use sandpaper to rub things until they are smooth.

Bumps on a tyre add friction, which helps grip a car to a road. The rubber on race car tyres is soft and sticky instead of bumpy.

Reducing friction

Objects have less friction if they are **rolled along**, rather than dragged. Slippery liquids can reduce friction, for example, between moving parts.

The brakes add friction to the wheel, making the bike slow down

Rolling wheels allow the bicycle to move over the ground

Oil helps the bike chain move smoothly

85

Gravity

When you jump up, why do you fall back down? The answer is gravity, a force that pulls everything towards the ground. Gravity exists around all objects. How strong it is depends on the **distance** between things and an object's **mass** — how much stuff it contains.

Discovering gravity
An English scientist called Isaac Newton figured out how gravity works in the late 1600s. He noticed an apple falling from a tree, and wondered why it had happened.

Gravity on Earth
Our planet is massive, so its gravity is **very strong**. It easily pulls small things towards the ground.

A kicked ball would fly forever without forces, such as gravity, acting on it.

Gravity in space

The Moon is like a big ball moving through space. **Earth's gravity pulls** on it, and stops it flying away.

The Moon has gravity, too, which pulls on Earth. This makes the sea rise and fall, causing tides.

This is the path that the Moon would naturally take.

This is the pull of the Moon and Earth on each other.

Moon

Earth

Earth's gravitational pull changes the natural path of the Moon.

For the same reason, Earth moves around the massive Sun.

The Moon moves around the Earth in a circular shape called an orbit.

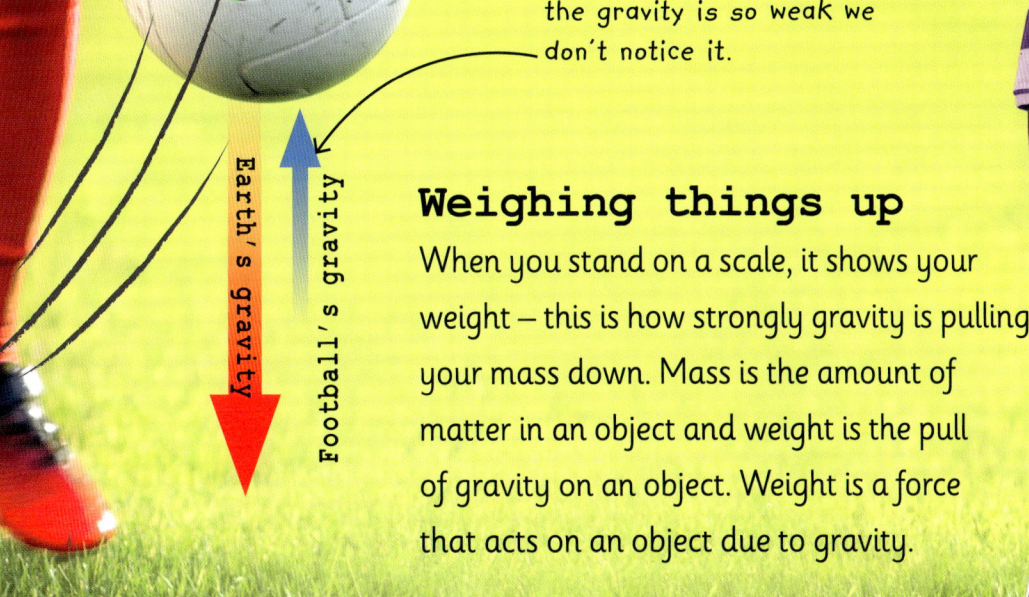

The ball has gravity, but it has very little mass, so the gravity is so weak we don't notice it.

Earth's gravity

Football's gravity

Weighing things up

When you stand on a scale, it shows your weight — this is how strongly gravity is pulling your mass down. Mass is the amount of matter in an object and weight is the pull of gravity on an object. Weight is a force that acts on an object due to gravity.

S-t-r-e-t-c-h and ... squash!

Bend
Bending means to **put a curve** into something. It can be useful for fitting something long into a small space.

Bending the paper gives the frog its legs.

Twist
Turning something to change its shape is called twisting. It can **make things stronger**.

Twist it!

Twisting threads makes a rope-like structure.

Fantastic elastic
Some materials can change shape and then **bounce back**! They are elastic.

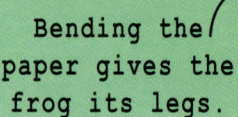

Elastic materials are made of long chains of coiled-up molecules. That's why they can be stretched out and spring back.

Coiled-up

Stretched out

You can use different forces to **change the shape** of materials and, sometimes, their use.

The glue in this slime makes it stretchy.

Squash
Squeezing or pressing something to **make it flatter** is called squashing.

Squeeeeze!

Squeezing an orange gives us juice.

Stretch
Stretching means to make something **wider** or **longer** by pulling.

S-t-r-e-t-c-h

Ka-POW!
Using force to stretch elastic materials **puts energy into them**. They store it until they are let go.

Energy out

Energy in

Energy stored in the stretched springs

Simple machines

Some machines are so basic you might not realize they are machines. A simple machine is a **mechanical device** that changes the direction or size of a force.

Even a swing is a machine, called a lever! Wheeeeee!

Wedge
Believe it or not, a **knife** is a simple machine, called a wedge. Like other wedges, it is thin at one edge, and thicker at the other. This helps it to **separate things** like food easily.

The fulcrum is the turning point.

Lever
If you **push down** on one end of a lever, the other end **goes up**. A seesaw is a lever — it has a long beam that turns on a fulcrum, or pivot. A lever helps you lift a big weight with less effort.

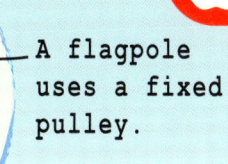

Pulley

How can you lift a heavy object up easily? Use a pulley, which is **a rope looped over a wheel**. Pull down on the rope to lift the object up. It's easier than pulling up as you can use your body weight to help pull down.

A flagpole uses a fixed pulley.

Pulley

Slope

In science, even a slope is a kind of machine. It's **easier to push things up** than lift them.

How many simple machines can you spot in this playground?

Screw

Turn a screw, and it **goes down**. This is because of its thread — a spiral pattern winding around it.

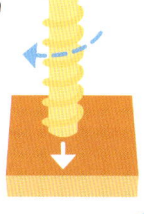

Screws are screwed in clockwise.

Wheel

Wheels help things **move along smoothly**. They are attached to a pole called an axle.

Turning the axle makes the wheels go around.

Axle

Engines

Engines **make things move**. Vehicles such as cars, trains, boats, planes, and rockets have them. Different engines work in different ways.

> Combustion engines produce DIRTY EXHAUST FUMES, but electric motors do not.

Combustion engine

Some vehicles use combustion engines. Fuel is to make an **explosive fire**. The explosion pushes a piston which turns a crankshaft that makes the wheels move.

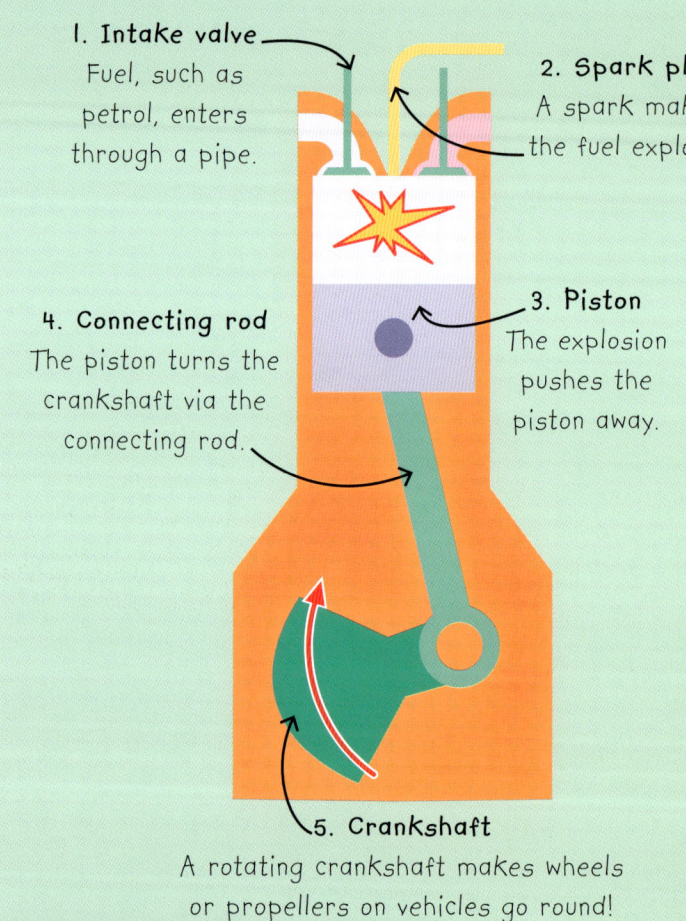

1. **Intake valve** Fuel, such as petrol, enters through a pipe.
2. **Spark plug** A spark makes the fuel explode.
3. **Piston** The explosion pushes the piston away.
4. **Connecting rod** The piston turns the crankshaft via the connecting rod.
5. **Crankshaft** A rotating crankshaft makes wheels or propellers on vehicles go round!

Early train engines used **steam** instead of fuel to push the pistons.

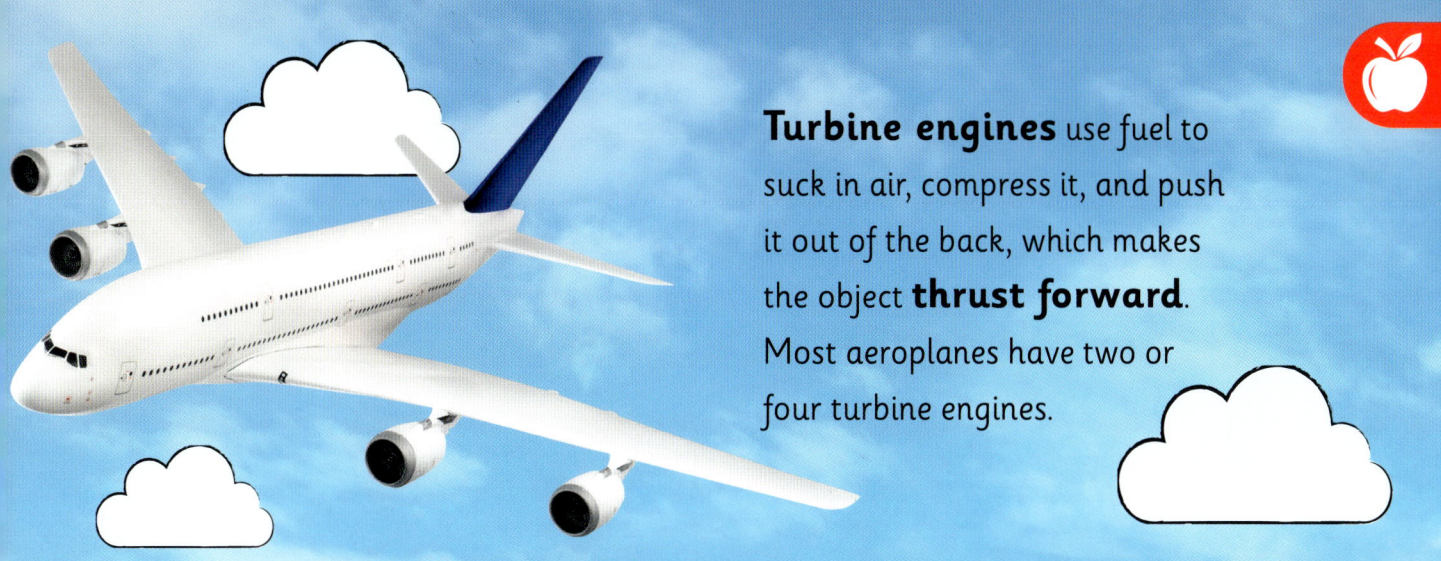

Turbine engines use fuel to suck in air, compress it, and push it out of the back, which makes the object **thrust forward**. Most aeroplanes have two or four turbine engines.

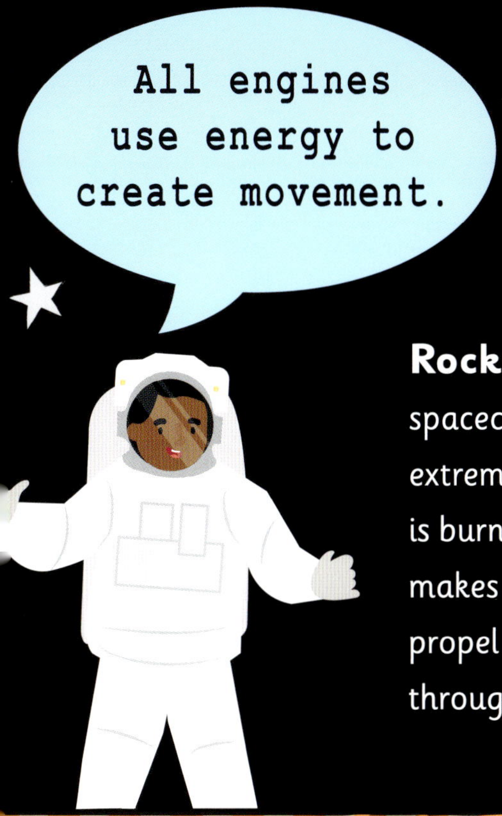

All engines use energy to create movement.

Rocket engines launch spacecraft into space. They are extremely powerful. Lots of fuel is burnt inside a chamber, which makes **hot gas** burst out and propel the rocket very quickly through the air.

Electric cars don't have engines. Instead, they use **electricity and magnetism** to power a motor, which makes the wheels turn.

93

Flying high

How can something as heavy as a plane fly up into the air? It's all to do with four forces: **lift, weight, thrust,** and **drag**.

When lift is greater than weight, the plane flies up!

Thrust

Engines and propellers whirr around. These push air backwards, making the plane thrust forward.

Planes have smooth, sleek shapes to cut through air and reduce drag.

Birds have not only inspired the design of planes, but trains, too. The kingfisher's beak inspired the design for the front and back of a bullet train.

Nature's fliers

Have you noticed that planes look a little like birds? It's the **same science** that makes them both fly. A bird's wing both **propels** and creates **lift**.

Up, up, and away

Balloons fly when they are filled with something **less dense** (packed together) than the air around them. Warm air is light so hot-air balloons rise.

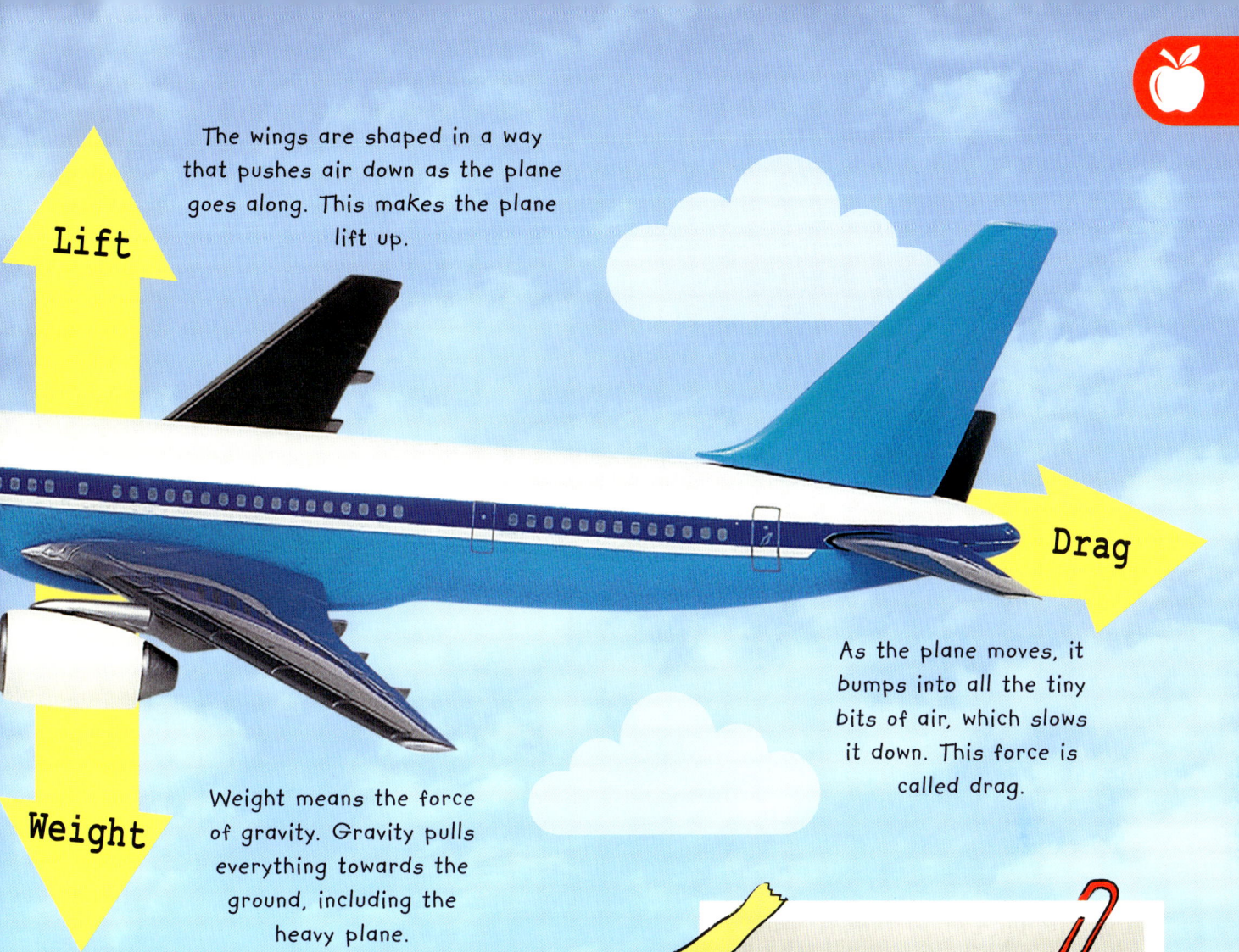

Lift — The wings are shaped in a way that pushes air down as the plane goes along. This makes the plane lift up.

Drag — As the plane moves, it bumps into all the tiny bits of air, which slows it down. This force is called drag.

Weight — Weight means the force of gravity. Gravity pulls everything towards the ground, including the heavy plane.

Chop, chop

The propellers on the tops of helicopters **push air down**, creating lots of lift. Helicopters can take off using thrust, which can be sidewards, forwards, vertical, or rearwards.

First flight

The first ever flight was made by two American brothers called Wilbur and Orville Wright, in 1903. Their plane **flew for 12 seconds**, over a distance of 37 metres (120 feet).

Pressure

Although you may not notice, whenever you **press or push** on something, you apply a force called pressure. The **bigger the force** — from kicking a ball to blowing a balloon — the **bigger the pressure.**

The air pressure inside a balloon is greater than the air outside of it.

Big snow shoes mean you won't sink in the snow! Your weight is spread out, and this lowers the pressure.

Under pressure
Pressure is the **force applied** to a specific area — and the size of the area matters. If you apply force to something big it spreads out, reducing the pressure. If you use the same force on a smaller thing, it stays only on this small area, which increases the pressure.

Bang!

Bang!

It's fun to jump into a pool and feel the force of the water. The weight of the water above you pushes down and piles pressure on your body. Submarines are designed with strong hulls to cope with the extreme pressure deep underwater.

Spray away

When you shake a can of spray paint, it mixes liquified gas with paint powder. When you press the top of the can, **pressure is released** and the liquified gas comes out. It expands rapidly into a gas, taking the paint powder with it.

Do your ears "pop" on a plane? It's a sensation caused by a change in air pressure. When an aircraft takes off or lands at high speed, a tube inside your ear sometimes opens with a pop sound to cope with the pressure and keep you comfortable.

On your bike

If you're going on a bike ride, you need to keep your tyres pumped full of air. When a tyre is full, the air has nowhere else to go. **Pressure builds up inside the tyre**, making it **strong** and **solid**. This compressed air helps you to cycle smoothly and speedily.

Bike pump

I thought it would float!

Floating and sinking

Colossal cruise ships are heavyweight **floating cities** that sail the seas without sinking. Yet if you stand on the ship's deck and toss a coin into the water, it **sinks** like a stone. Why? Let's dive in…

PLOP!

Density decider
The reason why something sinks or floats is to do with its density — the amount of material inside an object. Anything that is **less dense** than water **floats**, but anything **more dense** than water **sinks**. As a cruise ship is made up of a metal body with air inside it, its overall density is less than water. A coin is solid metal with no air inside. Its density is greater than water.

A coin is MORE DENSE than water.

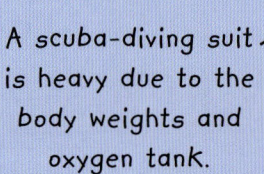

A scuba-diving suit is heavy due to the body weights and oxygen tank.

Anything that can float is described as buoyant.

Floating boats

The **sheer weight** of a cruise ship pushes some of the water aside. At the same time, the water below the ship pushes upwards on the boat, which is called **upthrust**. The cruise ship is less dense than the water and the upthrust is big enough to push up and make the ship float.

Life ring floating

Staying afloat

If you put an inflatable **life ring** around your middle, you will stay afloat in water because the air inside it makes you much less dense than water. If you wear a heavy **scuba-diving suit**, however, the total density will be more dense than the water, and you will sink down to the seabed.

Fish have the same density as water so they float within it.

Feel the force

Anything that goes into water experiences two different forces. There is the force that comes from the **object's weight** (as gravity pulls it down) and the **upthrust**. When the weight is the same as or less than the upthrust, the object floats. When the weight is more than the upthrust, the object sinks.

The weight of the brick pulls it down.

The weight of the duck pulls it down

Buoyancy pushes the duck up.

The upthrust is not strong enough to stop the brick from sinking.

Energy

Zoom! **Pop**! **Bang**! We can **see**, **hear**, and **feel** energy all around us. It's in **lights** and **sirens**, the **wind** and the **waves**, and even inside our **bodies**. But what actually is it, where does it come from, and where does it go?

SUN — What is energy?

Energy is what **makes everything happen**. In science, we think of it as the thing that makes it possible to do work.

The Sun

Our Sun gives out **huge amounts of energy** in the form of **heat and light**. The Sun's heat and light travel millions of miles through space to reach us.

The Sun gives plants ENERGY TO GROW.

Energy cannot be destroyed, only MOVED from place to place.

Movement
The food you eat gives your body the energy it needs to move around. You turn the **food energy into movement energy**, allowing you to stand, walk, and run.

Food
Plants use the **Sun's light** to make energy for themselves. When animals eat plants, the **plants' energy is transferred** to them. The energy gets passed on again if an animal is then eaten by another animal.

Food gives animals ENERGY TO MOVE.

Types of energy

Energy comes in many forms. Some types keep energy **in one place**, others move it **from place to place** or between objects.

Potential

Some things store energy, and can **release the energy later**. This is called potential energy.

Electrical

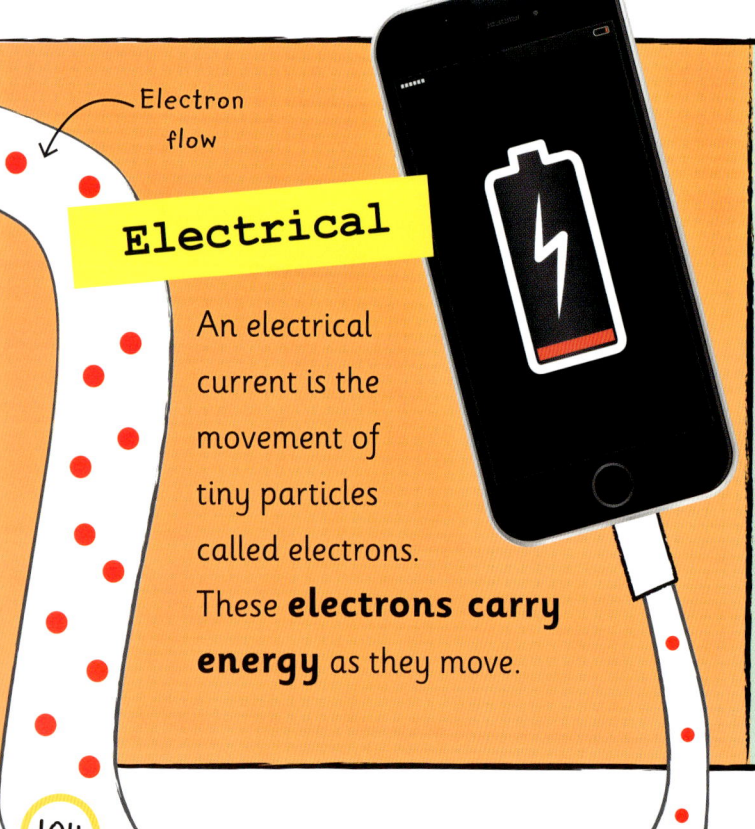

Electron flow

An electrical current is the movement of tiny particles called electrons. These **electrons carry energy** as they move.

Chemical

Chemical energy is the energy stored in the **bonds** between **particles** in chemicals. When energy is used up, these bonds are broken. Chemical energy must be converted into another form of energy to be used.

Batteries store chemical energy.

Food is a store of chemical energy.

Chemical energy in FOOD is

Steam from a kettle full of boiling water

Heat

Things have different amounts of energy depending on how hot or cold they are. **Hot things** have **more energy** than cold things.

Light

Light is the only energy we can see.

Light is a form of energy that moves in waves. It **travels in straight lines**, very fast.

Movement

Moving objects have **"kinetic" energy**.

Nuclear

Everything around us is made of tiny building blocks called **atoms**. If those atoms are smashed apart, they create **huge amounts of energy**, which we call nuclear energy.

Sound

The sounds we hear are a type of energy, which moves in **waves**. **Air particles** are **squeezed** and **stretched** as a sound wave travels through them.

Sound waves

changed into mechanical energy, which makes muscles move.

Energy on the move

Everything that moves has movement energy, which we also call **kinetic** energy. Things that aren't moving, but could or are about to, have **potential** energy.

Whooosh!

Kinetic energy

We have kinetic (**movement**) energy as we move around. Kinetic energy can also be **passed** between things:

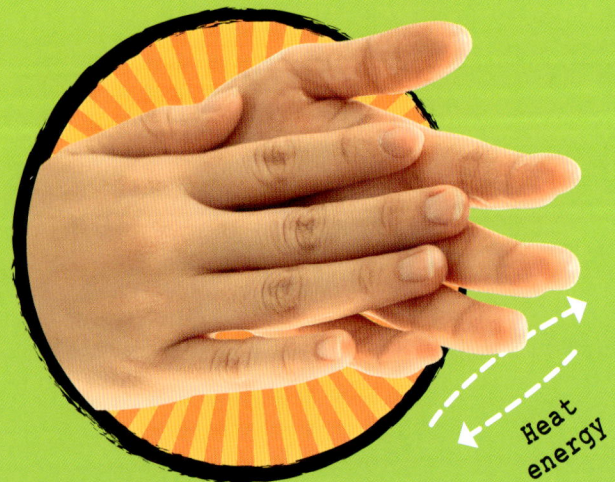

Rubbing your hands together transfers kinetic energy into heat energy.

Kicking a ball moves energy from your foot to the ball.

The FASTER something goes,

Potential energy

This type of energy is currently **not doing any work** – but it could be. It has potential, so we call it potential energy.

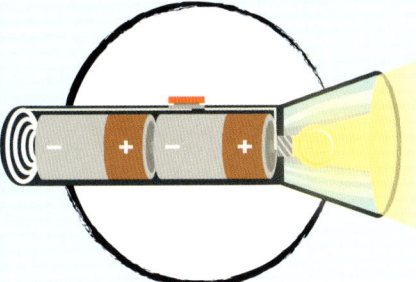

Electrical
Batteries contain a **store of energy** that can be let out as electrical current (moving electricity).

Elastic
Stretching and squashing can release potential energy when a thing **springs back** to its original shape.

Falling
Anything high up has the potential to fall down. Once it falls, it is moving, and has **kinetic energy**.

Changing energy

A roller-coaster uses **kinetic** and **potential** energy to give people a fun ride! It has potential energy when it is high up and kinetic energy when it moves downhill.

High up, the roller-coaster car has lots of potential energy.

Downhill, the car has kinetic energy.

The car will stop when all of its energy is transformed into friction and air resistance.

ZOOOOM....

the MORE KINETIC ENERGY it has.

Wave after wave

Everyone loves a day at the seaside! You can play in the sand and jump in the waves that crash against the shore. There are **other waves** around, too, but you **don't see them** in the same way …

Infrared waves

We cannot see infrared light waves, but we can **feel the waves** as heat from the Sun on our skin. It is estimated that more than half of the Sun's radiation is infrared.

Ultraviolet (UV) waves

It's important to wear sun cream, a hat, and sunglasses on a sunny day. That's because ultraviolet waves from the Sun **cause sunburn**. They can also lead to wrinkles and they play a part in some skin cancers.

Humans can't see UV waves, but bees can!

The higher the sun protection factor (SPF) number, the more you are protected.

Measuring wavelengths

The **highest point** of a wave is called the crest, while the **lowest point** is called a trough. A wavelength is the distance between the crest of a wave and the crest of the next wave or the distance between the trough of a wave and the trough of the next wave.

Some waves are made by wind, but swell waves happen because of energy beneath the ocean surface.

Heat

Heat is a **kind of energy**. You can feel it coming out of **the Sun**, a **fire**, or even your own **body**!

The science of heat
Atoms move around. **Cold atoms** have less energy and move slowly. **Heating** atoms gives them energy and they move faster.

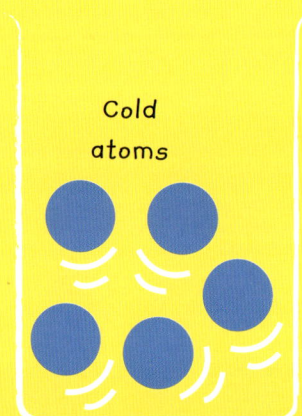
Cold atoms

Hot atoms

Absolute zero temperature is -273.15°C (-459.67°F).

How hot?
We measure heat as **temperature**. The higher the temperature, the hotter a thing is.

Antarctic ice
-89.22°C (-128.6°F)

Ice cream
-15°C (5°F)

Seeing heat

Heat travels in invisible **infrared rays**. Special cameras can detect infrared rays and show us pictures of heat. Different colours show how hot or cold something is.

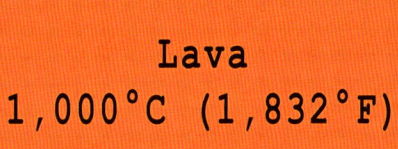

Hot areas are shown in red.

Hot chocolate
70°C (158°F)

Lava
1,000°C (1,832°F)

Surface of the Sun
5,500°C (10,000°F)

Hotter and colder

Heat is always **on the move** and goes from warmer things to colder things. It travels in three ways: conduction, convection, and radiation.

Conduction

Heat can **move through** materials, transferring heat from particle to particle. That's why a frying pan – and whatever is inside – gets hot.

Convection

Hot liquids and gases rise above cooler ones. If you keep heating a liquid or a gas from below, it will all warm up.

The hotter liquid (or gas) rises to the surface allowing cooler parts to warm up.

Polar bears have up to 11 cm (4 in) of fat and 15 cm (6 in) of fur.

The fur, feathers, and fat of birds and mammals trap heat, keeping the animal warm. Trapping heat is called insulation.

Radiation

The Sun radiates heat and light, which is why our world is warm. Hot things radiate heat and **warm up the air** nearby.

Heat is trapped between layers of clothes.

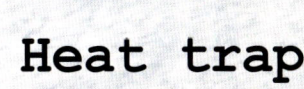

Heat trap

On a cold day, heat moves from our warm bodies into the air. The clothes we wear stop the warm air from escaping. If it does escape, our bodies **use more energy** to heat up the cold air that replaces it.

How it works

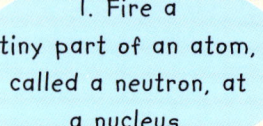

1. Fire a tiny part of an atom, called a neutron, at a nucleus.

Nucleus

Neutrons and energy are released.

The nucleus splits in two.

Neutron

2. The nucleus splits, releasing more neutrons and energy!

Divided nucleus

Nuclear energy

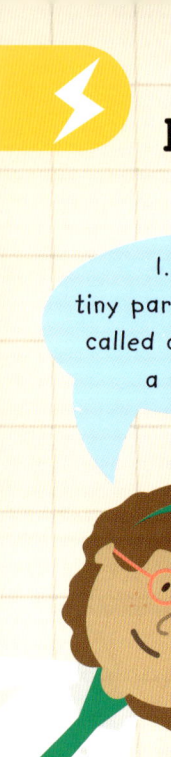

Inside an atom is a **nucleus**. **Splitting** a nucleus apart can release huge amounts of energy, called nuclear energy.

Nuclear power station

Using nuclear energy

The **heat** that is created from the reaction is used to boil water into steam. The steam drives turbines, which **generate electricity**.

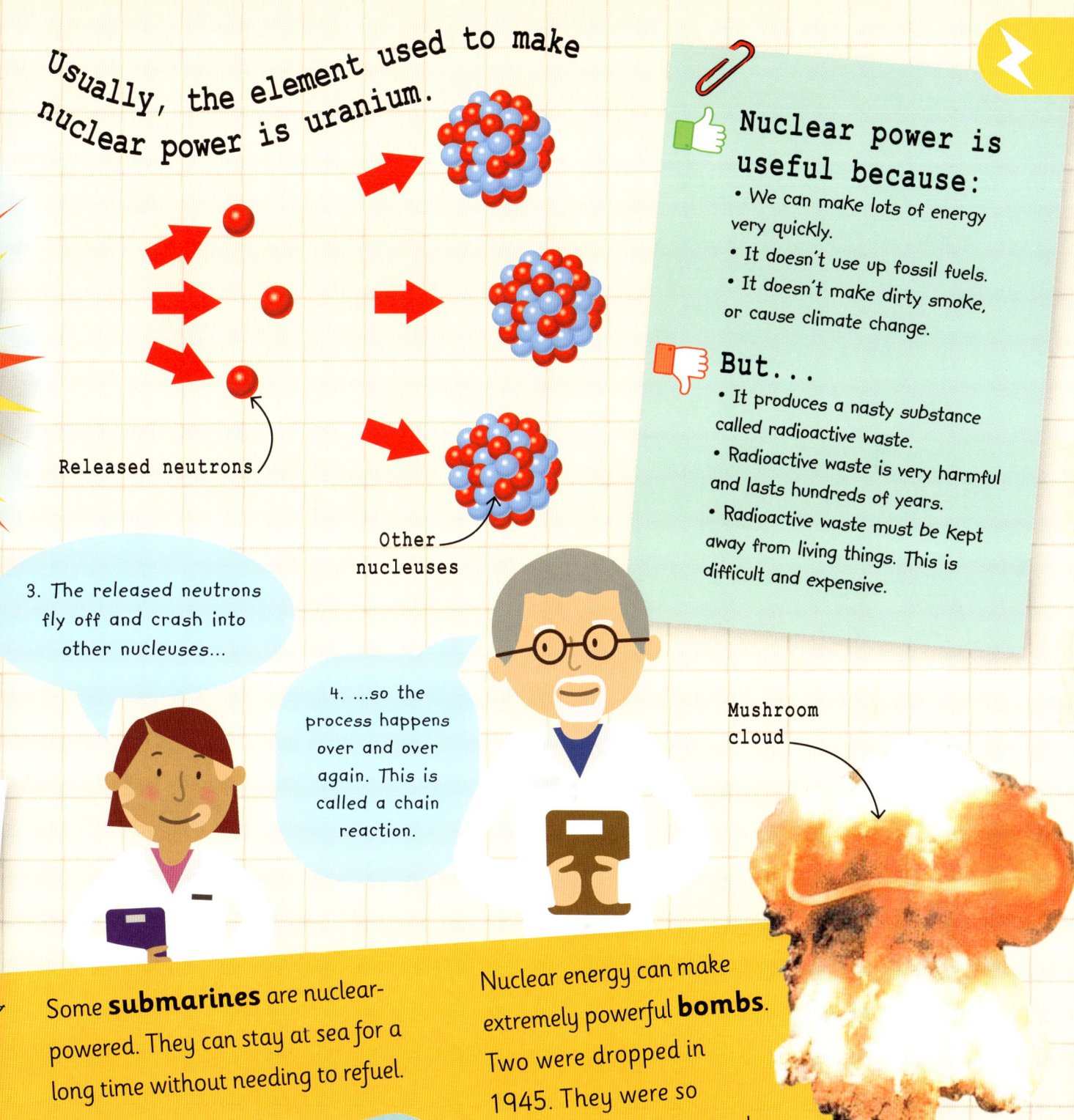

Usually, the element used to make nuclear power is uranium.

Released neutrons

Other nucleuses

3. The released neutrons fly off and crash into other nucleuses...

4. ...so the process happens over and over again. This is called a chain reaction.

Nuclear power is useful because:
- We can make lots of energy very quickly.
- It doesn't use up fossil fuels.
- It doesn't make dirty smoke, or cause climate change.

But...
- It produces a nasty substance called radioactive waste.
- Radioactive waste is very harmful and lasts hundreds of years.
- Radioactive waste must be kept away from living things. This is difficult and expensive.

Mushroom cloud

Some **submarines** are nuclear-powered. They can stay at sea for a long time without needing to refuel.

Submarine

Nuclear energy can make extremely powerful **bombs**. Two were dropped in 1945. They were so terrible that people agreed **never** to use them again.

Changing energies

Energy cannot be **destroyed**, but it can change from one **form** to another.

1. Light energy travels from the Sun to Earth.

2. Plants use light to grow. They change light energy into chemical energy.

Natural changes
Energy is constantly **changing form** in the natural world.

3. The stored chemical energy in plants is passed on to animals, including us, when we eat plants.

4. Chemical reactions from the food we eat create heat energy that we use to stay warm.

5. Chemical reactions also create mechanical energy that we need to do work or activities.

Energy inventions

People have created machines that **transform** energy, so that it can be **useful**.

At its highest point, the ball's kinetic energy has become potential energy.

The ball has a moving energy called kinetic energy.

Throwing the ball in the air uses mechanical energy.

Waterwheel
Rushing water turns a wheel, which powers machines, such as grinders and pumps.

Engine
Burning fuel releases the energy stored inside it, which can be used to make wheels turn.

Light bulb
When we switch on a lamp, electrical energy flows into the bulb and makes it light up. This energy becomes light energy.

Electric turbine
Kinetic energy, such as wind, can be transformed into electric energy by a generator.

Television
Televisions turn electrical energy into light and sound.

Sounds good

When a dog barks its vocal chords move, causing **vibrations**. Vibrations travel through air around a moving thing, creating waves of sound.

Woof! Woof!

Sound waves

Sounds get QUIETER as

Waves on the move
Sound waves travel through **solids and liquids** as well as **air**. For example, they can travel through water and wood.

Blue whales can make sounds as loud as a jet plane.

There is NO AIR in space, which means it is silent –

...they TRAVEL AWAY from where they started.

Sound bounces off a wall...
...and is reflected back.

Brrrrring!!

Bouncing sound
Sound waves travel in **straight lines**. If they bump into something, sound can **bounce** back, changing direction.

How loud?
Small vibrations make small waves and big vibrations make big waves. The **bigger** the wave, the **louder** the sound that comes with it.

Small, shallow wave

Rustling leaves

Bigger wave

Strummed guitar

Large, deep wave

Racing car

because sound needs air to travel through.

Light

We see everything in our world because of light. It is a type of **energy**, which fills our world with beautiful colour!

Rainbow colours

The light we see is called **white light**. It is made up of seven colours — the colours of the rainbow.

One colour becomes seven

Light bends, or refracts

Light travels in a straight line

Glass prism

In the shadows

A shadow is formed when **light is blocked** by an object. The shadow takes on the shape of the object blocking the light.

The closer the object is to the light, the bigger the shadow.

Making light

Light can come from a number of sources.

Light bulbs and **candles** give off light.

Reflection

Light can bounce off surfaces. It bounces off **shiny surfaces**, such as water and glass, the most. This bouncing is called reflection.

Light reflecting off water

We SEE light using our EYES.

The **Sun** shines constantly, filling the world with light.

Some **animals** can create their own light.

Glow-worm

Seeing colour

The colours people see around them are caused by **light bouncing back** off objects. If an object reflects only green light, the object will appear green.

Sunlight

Green light reflects into the eyes

The apple's skin absorbs every colour except for green.

Colour

Colour is seen when **light shines off** an object. The science of colour is called chromatics.

The Sun's rays
Sunlight looks white, but it is really a spectrum (range) of colours. In 1672, English scientist Isaac Newton discovered the **spectrum of seven colours** – red, orange, yellow, green, blue, indigo, and violet. Scientists now understand there are millions, and possibly an infinite number, of colours.

RED
ORANGE
YELLOW
GREEN
BLUE
INDIGO
VIOLET

Raindrop

Isaac Newton with his telescope

Rainbows
Raindrops work like prisms in the natural world. When **sunlight is refracted and reflected off a raindrop**, each colour in the light bends by a different amount, and the colours become separated, forming a rainbow.

Bees can see a type of light called ultraviolet, which is invisible to us.

Refraction

Light travels in a straight line, but it can **bend**. This is called refraction. When a ray of light travels through a transparent material, like **water** or **glass**, it slows down and bends in a different direction. Lenses for glasses use refraction.

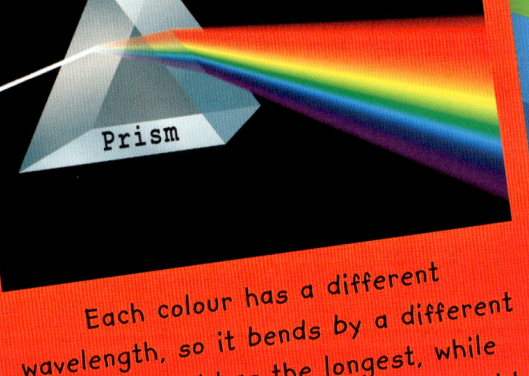

Each colour has a different wavelength, so it bends by a different amount. Red has the longest, while violet has the shortest. A ray of light can be passed through a 3-D object called a glass prism. The prism bends each colour by a different amount, and the colours separate out.

Moonbow

Rarer than a rainbow, a MOONBOW occurs when sunlight is reflected by the Moon and reflected and refracted by raindrops.

123

Reflections

A mirror reveals your true reflection. This **super-smooth** surface **bounces** back patterns of light to make your image **clear**. It provides an instant way to check how you're looking!

Most surfaces **absorb** light as it hits them. But mirrors **reflect** most of the light. We see a regular reflection when light is bounced back from a flat shiny surface into our eyes in an orderly way.

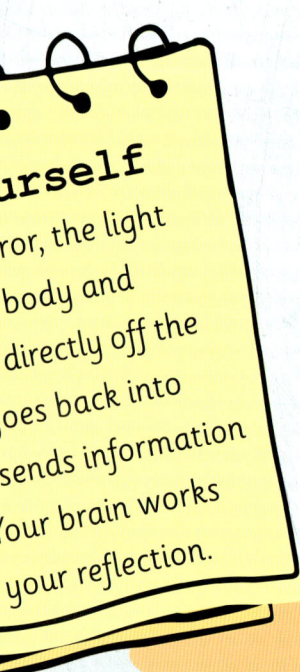

See for yourself

If you look in a mirror, the light reflecting off your body and clothes **reflects** directly off the glass. This light goes back into your **eyes** and sends information to the **brain**. Your brain works out that this is your reflection.

Mirror

Reflection

Smooth the way

Smooth, **shiny** surfaces are best for reflections because they reflect the most light. This light bounces off in an orderly way in the same direction. This is called **specular reflection**.

In the rough

Rough surfaces cannot create good reflections. Instead, light is **scattered** far and wide in all different directions. This is called **diffuse reflection**.

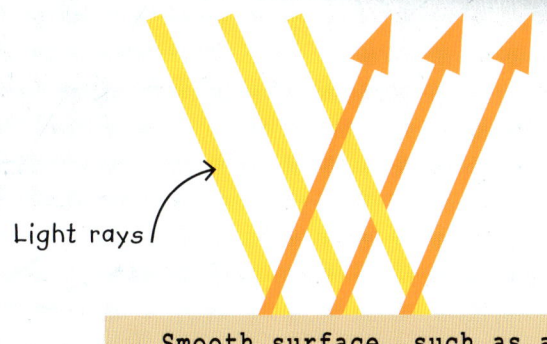

Light rays

Smooth surface, such as a mirror or polished metal.

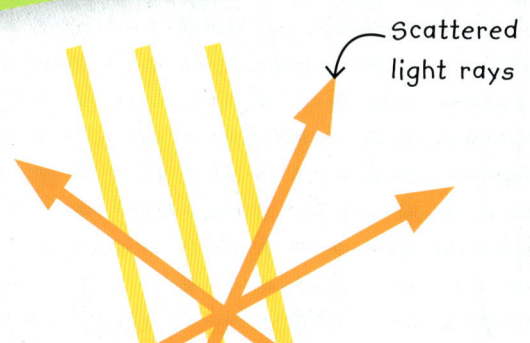

Scattered light rays

Rough surface, such as a wall or table.

Altered images

Concave mirrors curve in at the middle, which makes objects appear upside down at a distance, but stretched bigger and the right way up at close range. **Convex mirrors** curve out in the middle to make objects look smaller and more squashed than they are.

Concave mirror

Convex mirror

3-D images

In 1980, US-born scientist **Valerie Thomas** invented an illusion transmitter after experimenting with concave mirrors. Valerie's invention sends an optical illusion of a 3D image that appears to be real. NASA still use her technology today.

125

Refraction

Light usually whizzes about in **straight lines**, but it can also **bend** in a process called refraction. Here is how you can see refraction in action.

Refracted light rays

Speed of light
Light travels at different **speeds** depending on what it is **passing through**. Most of the time, light passes through air at high speed. When light reaches a see-through substance, like water or glass, it slows down and changes direction by bending.

Refraction experiment
Stand a pencil in a glass of water. The pencil appears **bent** at the surface where it passes from the **air** to the **water**. The light travels more slowly through water than air so the angle of the light changes. The light changes speed as it enters the air again, causing another bend.

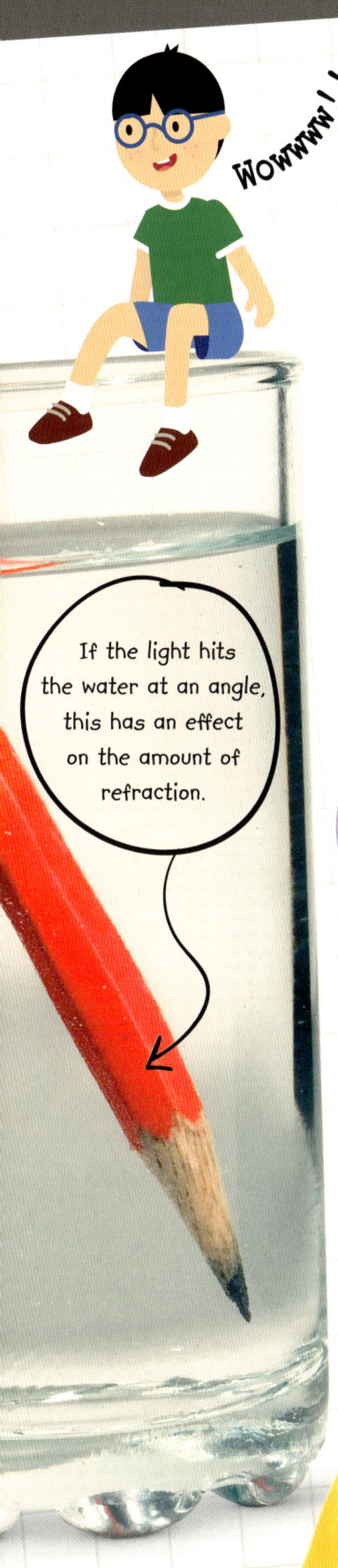

If the light hits the water at an angle, this has an effect on the amount of refraction.

Trick of the light

The pencil isn't really bent – the image is just how our **eyes** see the change in light speed. This is called an **optical illusion**. The same is true if you look at a fish in water. Light travels more slowly in water than in air so the fish looks like it's in a different position from where it actually is.

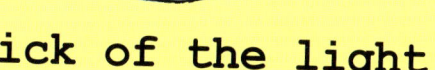

Wowww!!

Observer

Light ray in air

Light ray in water

Fish appears here

Actual position of fish

Some people need GLASSES to see things far away or close up.

Helping hand

Refraction can be used to improve problems with **vision**. **Glasses** and **contact lenses** bend light rays coming into the eyes to either **magnify** (make bigger) or **reduce** (make smaller) the view. This brings the image into focus in your eye so it can be seen clearly.

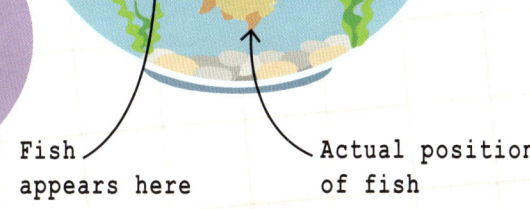

Contact lenses

A closer look

We use telescopes to look more closely at **objects that are far away**. The first telescopes were simple and small enough to be **held in the hand**. Today, telescopes can be as **tall as skyscrapers**!

The first telescopes were made more than 400 years ago.

Large radio telescope

Small telescope

See it all
To get a good view of objects that are far away in our **Solar System**, scientists use supersized telescopes. These large telescopes contain giant mirrors to collect huge amounts of light.

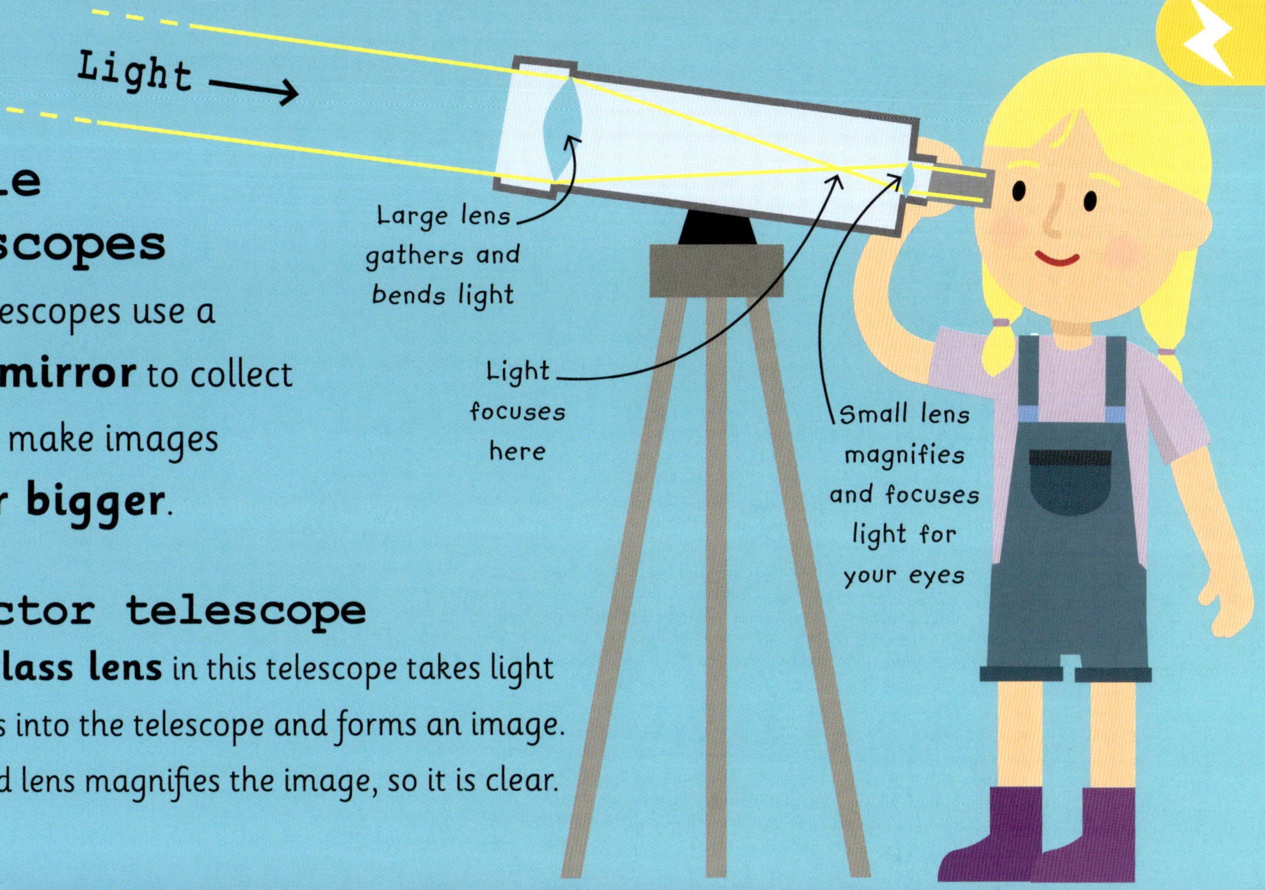

Simple telescopes

These telescopes use a **lens** or **mirror** to collect light and make images **appear bigger**.

Refractor telescope

The first **glass lens** in this telescope takes light that shines into the telescope and forms an image. The second lens magnifies the image, so it is clear.

Light →

Large lens gathers and bends light

Light focuses here

Small lens magnifies and focuses light for your eyes

Space telescopes

The latest telescopes send us **detailed pictures** of space objects that are billions of light years away! They are **positioned in space**, so that their views are not blocked by clouds in Earth's atmosphere.

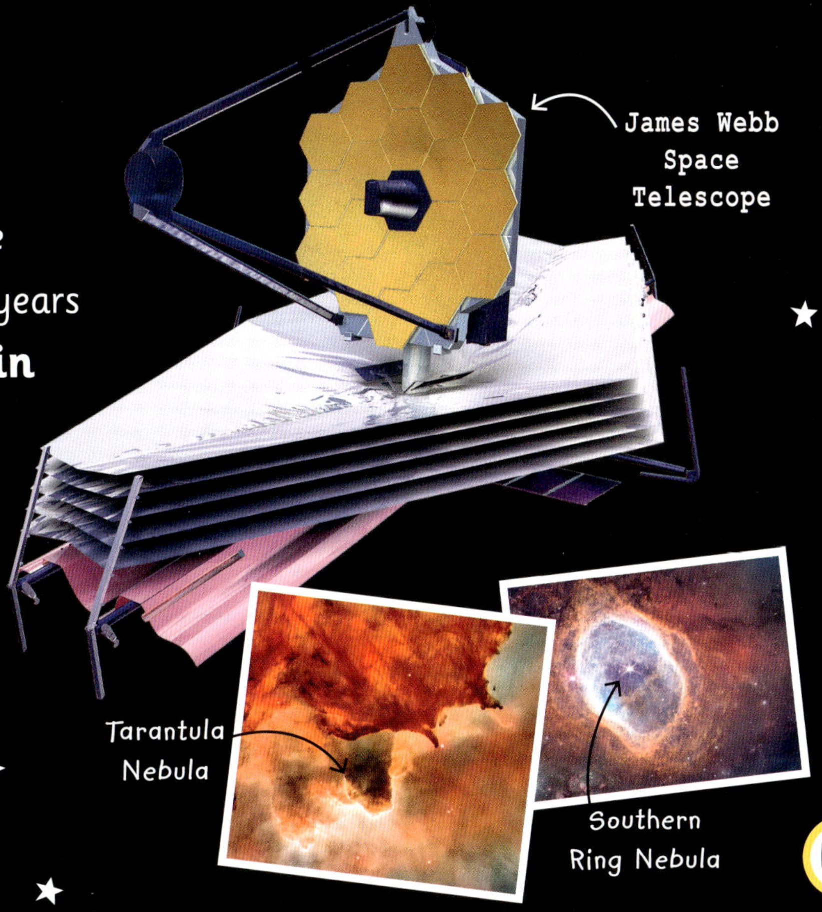

James Webb Space Telescope

Tarantula Nebula

Southern Ring Nebula

129

and magnets

"I am Sophia. I was invented in 2016, and am the first robot to have my own passport!"

Electricity and magnetism are **two forms** of energy that we have learned to use in many different ways. Electricity **lights up** our world, while magnetism can be **used to lift** heavy objects and help trains zoom along tracks **faster** than ever before.

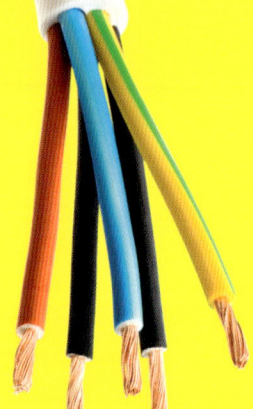

Electric wires
Electricity **travels through** certain types of **metal**. We use metal wires to direct electricity to our homes.

Electricity

Electricity is a **type of energy**. We use it to make all sorts of different things work, including machines and lights.

Electricity powers almost every appliance in the world around us!

Using electricity
Pretty much everything we **turn on and off** needs electricity to work. Some items must be plugged into a supply of electricity, others have batteries inside them.

Tablet
Tablets have **internal batteries** that can be **recharged** from a power supply, such as a wall socket or power bank.

Making electricity

We make electricity from other types of energy. For example, **wind** has **movement energy**. If it turns a turbine, the wind's movement energy can be turned into electrical energy.

Electricity has always existed, but it wasn't used in our homes until the 19th century.

Light bulb

Lights shines when **electricity runs through** a light bulb. Bulbs are usually plugged into an electricity supply, but some, such as torches, have batteries.

TV

Televisions are usually plugged into an **electrical socket**.

Circuits

A circuit is a **loop** that electrical energy can flow around. A complete circuit has a supply of energy, such as a **battery**, and **wires** to connect it together. Other things can be added too, such as light bulbs and on-off switches.

Using an on-off switch

click!

Power source
For electricity to **move around a circuit** it needs a power source. This is often a battery.

Electricity is a type of energy.

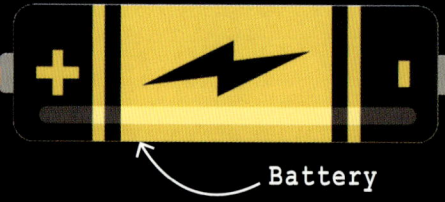

Battery

Wires
Everything in a circuit has to be **linked** for it to work. It is connected by copper wires through which electricity can flow. The wires are **covered in plastic** to prevent electricity flowing through our bodies if we touch them. Plastic is an insulator – it doesn't allow electricity to flow through it.

Copper wires

A flow of electricity is called a current.

Light bulb

A light bulb **shines** when electricity flows through it. This is useful in a circuit, because it shows if a circuit is working!

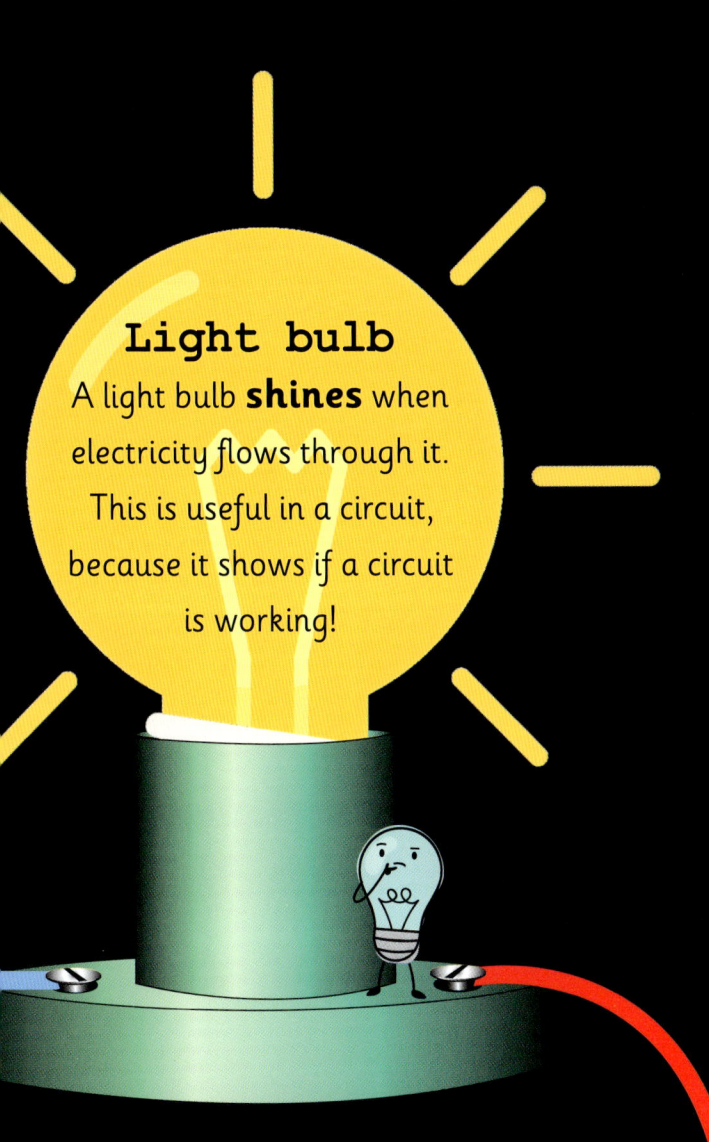

Switch

A switch can be used to turn a circuit **on or off**. When it is on, the circuit is complete and electricity can move around it. When it is off, there is a break in the circuit, which stops the electricity flowing.

Types of circuits

Electric circuits can be designed in different ways. Here are **two ways** of setting up a simple circuit containing a battery and two bulbs.

Series circuit

In a series circuit, the current flows through each light bulb in turn. Some fairy lights are series circuits.

Parallel circuit

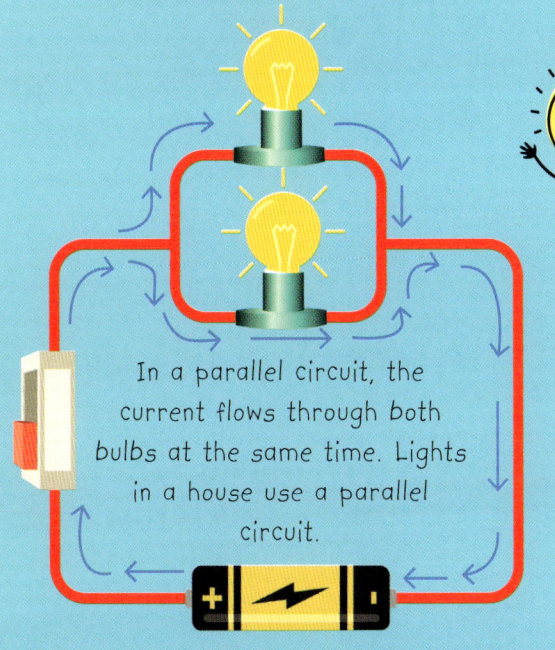

In a parallel circuit, the current flows through both bulbs at the same time. Lights in a house use a parallel circuit.

Static electricity

Electricity doesn't always flow – it can also **build up** in one place. When this happens we say there is "static" (**still**) electricity. Static electricity can build up naturally, but we can also create it.

Lightening bolt
When tiny particles rub together in clouds, they create a build-up of static electricity. Lightning bolts form when there is so much static electricity that it **jumps between clouds**, or down to the ground.

If you see LIGHTNING, it is best to stay indoors.

Plasma ball

A plasma ball creates static electricity, too, but at a smaller scale than lightning. The electricity **builds up** in the middle, then **zaps out** to the edges.

Van de Graaff generator

Unlike a plasma ball, a Van de Graaff generator creates static electricity that **flows out** into the environment. It can even make your hair rise!

Making static

We can create static electricity by **rubbing certain surfaces together**. Rubbing a blown-up balloon on your hair creates static, and your hair will be attracted to the balloon.

Negative charges attract positive charges

Magnets

A magnet is a special **metal** object with a super-strong attraction (pull) to an object that is magnetic. This **force** may be invisible, but you can certainly see the results of it in an instant when you use a magnet!

Magnetic field

The attraction between a magnet and an object is called a "magnetic field". Everything magnetic in this area is **drawn to the magnet**. You can feel this when you stick a magnet on a fridge and it stays in place.

Opposites attract

Every magnet has a **north pole** and a **south pole**. If two magnets are placed near each other with the opposite poles facing, the north pole of one is attracted to the south pole of the other. Their magnetic fields pull together and the magnets join.

North   South

Forced apart

If two magnets are placed with their north poles facing each other, the north pole of one is **repelled** (pushed back) by the north pole of the other. The same happens with the south poles. It is impossible to push the magnets together.

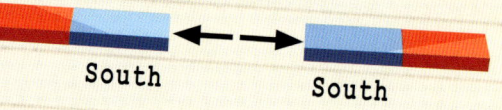

South   South

 Iron
 Cobalt
 Nickel

Magnetic metals

Not every metal is magnetic. The three magnetic metals are iron, cobalt, and nickel. **Steel** is made up of **different metals**, but because one of these metals is iron, steel is magnetic.

Explore your house with a magnet to see what you can attract and repel.

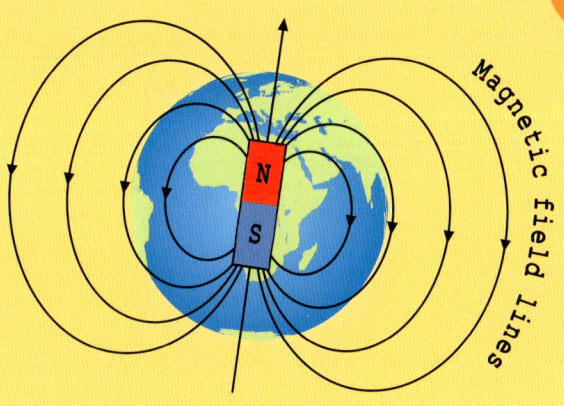

Magnetic field lines

Planet magnet

Earth is a huge magnet that produces its own magnetic field. This comes from **molten iron** moving around in our planet's outer core. One end of a compass needle always points north because of the pull of Earth's magnetic north pole.

Using a compass helps travellers navigate in the correct direction.

All aglow

The incredible natural light show, known as the Northern Lights, is created by solar winds and the Earth's magnetic field.

Electromagnets

Electricity and **magnetism** are incredibly powerful on their own, but when they come together, amazing things happen. Electromagnetism is put to good in many ways.

In action
An electromagnet can be made by wrapping a piece of **iron** in **wire**. When electricity is run through the wire via a **battery**, a magnetic field is created and metal objects are attracted to the iron rod.

Instant connection
Until the 19th century, experts thought electricity and magnetism were **separate things**. Danish scientist Hans Christian Ørsted found the connection when he turned on an electric current and a nearby compass needle jumped!

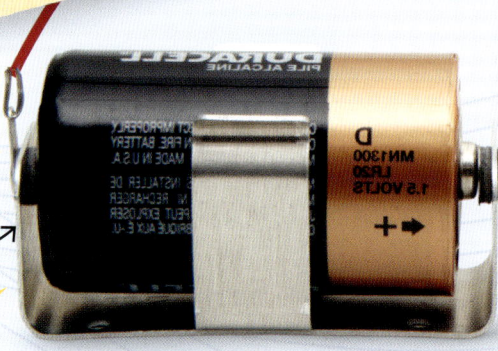

- Magnetized needle in a compass
- Wire
- The iron rod becomes a magnet.
- Switching off the current would stop the magnetic field.

Feel the force

Electromagnets can be **made stronger**, unlike other magnets. The more current that runs through the wire, the more powerful the electromagnet becomes. It is made even more powerful if more wire is wrapped around the iron.

When particles from the Sun collide with Earth's magnetic field, we see the Northern Lights.

Cranes pick up and carry heavy loads of scrap metal with powerful electromagnets.

Headphones, speakers, electric guitars, and even doorbells use electromagnets!

Rapid railways

Maglev trains use electromagnets on **train** and **track** to reach speeds of 600 kph (370 mph)! The magnets **repel** each other creating a gap between the train and track. This reduces friction and allows the train to go at a fast speed.

Maglev train

141

Using electricity

In the modern world, electricity is **all around us**. We use it to light our rooms, power machines, to make transport run, and so much more!

Circuits

Electricity flows along in one direction. To get it to go where we want, we use **wires, connected into loops** called circuits. A circuit needs a power source, such as a battery, to work. A light bulb is often powered by a simple circuit. Our electronic gadgets use more complicated circuits.

We have been using LIGHT BULBS

At home

Almost all the gadgets and machines in your home need electricity to make them work. Houses usually have two different types of **electric circuits**: one for the lights and one for everything else. Here are a few examples of things you might recognize in the home that use electricity.

Thermostat
Smart shower
Fridge freezer
Extractor hood
Microwave oven
Washing machine

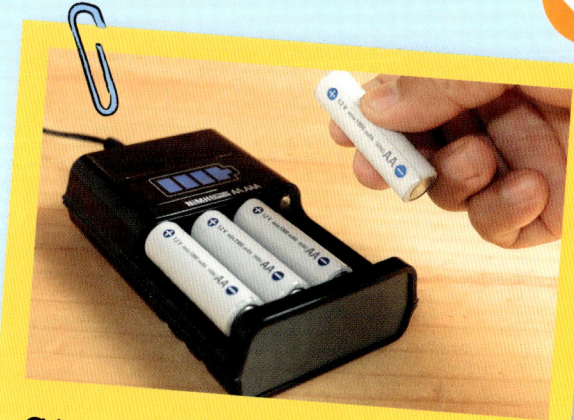

Storing power

Batteries **make electricity using chemicals**. They allow us to store electricity and use it without plugging a device into a power socket. Some batteries can be recharged.

On the move

Car engines are usually powered by **liquid fuel**, such as diesel or petrol. However, there are also electric cars, which are powered by **batteries** that can be recharged.

for more than 100 YEARS!

143

Supplying electricity

Electricity is made from sources such as coal and wind. Electricity travels through **wires** and **cables** to get to where we need it. The electricity's pressure (voltage) in the wires is dangerous.

Wind and solar energy are renewable energy sources.

Joining it up

A power network connects the places where **electricity is made** to the places where **it is used**.

Power station

1 **Electricity** is made in power stations.

	Coal	Oil	Nuclear
PROS 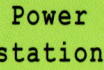	Coal is **cheap** and there is quite a lot available.	Oil is a **reliable** energy source.	Nuclear energy is cheap and even more reliable and **efficient** than coal or oil.
CONS 	Burning coal can pollute soil, air, and water. Carbon dioxide is also released, which adds to climate change. Coal will eventually **run out**.	Oil **pollutes** the air. Once it's used up, we can't get any more.	It makes **radioactive waste**, which is very dangerous to humans, animals, and the environment.

Most countries have their own power networks.

Power cuts
If something **goes wrong** in a power network, it can cause a power cut, and no electricity will be available. Power cuts can sometimes be **caused by storms**.

2 Networks of wires carry the electricity from the power stations to where it's needed. The wires are either carried **above ground**, on pylons, or are buried **underground**.

Pylon

3 We use the electricity in our **homes** and **workplaces**. Some places, such as factories, need more electricity than others, such as houses.

Underground cables

Wind	Tidal	Solar
Wind energy is **clean**, cheap to run, and renewable.	This renewable energy doesn't release gases that damage the environment. It is easy to **predict and track**.	**Renewable** Solar energy doesn't pollute the environment, it's silent, and there's plenty of it!
It is not continuously available, so can be **unreliable**. It is noisy and costs a lot to set up.	It is **expensive** and the equipment that is used has to be based near the shore. It can disturb fish when they need to migrate.	Using solar panels requires a **lot of space**. Harmful gases are produced when the panels are made.

Sun power
The Sun sends out **huge amounts of energy**, which we receive as sunlight. Sunlight allows plants to grow, and lights our world.

Renewable power
There is only a limited amount of fossil fuel left. However, there are types of energy that **won't run out**: solar (from the Sun), water, and wind.

One wind turbine can make enough electricity for 300 homes!

Wind can be used to turn spinning blades and produce electricity.

We use **solar panels** to catch the Sun's energy and turn it into electricity.

Water flowing down rivers or back and forth as tides can also be used to make electricity.

Energy sources

Energy is the **ability to do work**. There are many types of energy, and we use them to do lots of different things, such as heating our homes, cooking food, and powering factories.

At the moment, 75 PER CENT of our energy is not renewable.

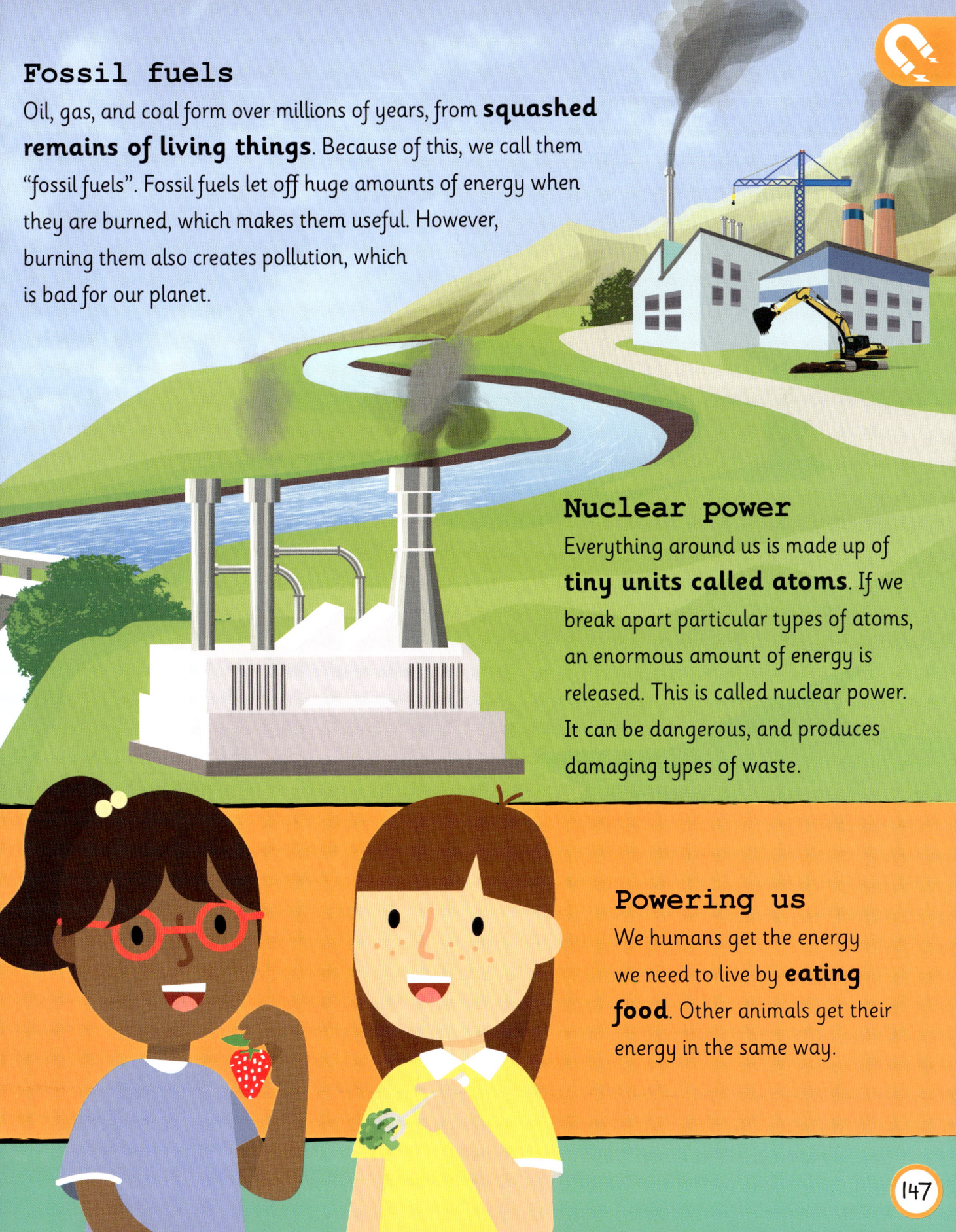

Fossil fuels

Oil, gas, and coal form over millions of years, from **squashed remains of living things**. Because of this, we call them "fossil fuels". Fossil fuels let off huge amounts of energy when they are burned, which makes them useful. However, burning them also creates pollution, which is bad for our planet.

Nuclear power

Everything around us is made up of **tiny units called atoms**. If we break apart particular types of atoms, an enormous amount of energy is released. This is called nuclear power. It can be dangerous, and produces damaging types of waste.

Powering us

We humans get the energy we need to live by **eating food**. Other animals get their energy in the same way.

Electronics

Electricity is a flow of energy that we use to **power things**, such as lights. Electronics are ways we control things that use electricity. They usually use tiny amounts of electricity, in a controlled way.

Electronics everywhere!
Most **high-tech devices** we use depend on electronics. These include mobile phones, computers, and televisions.

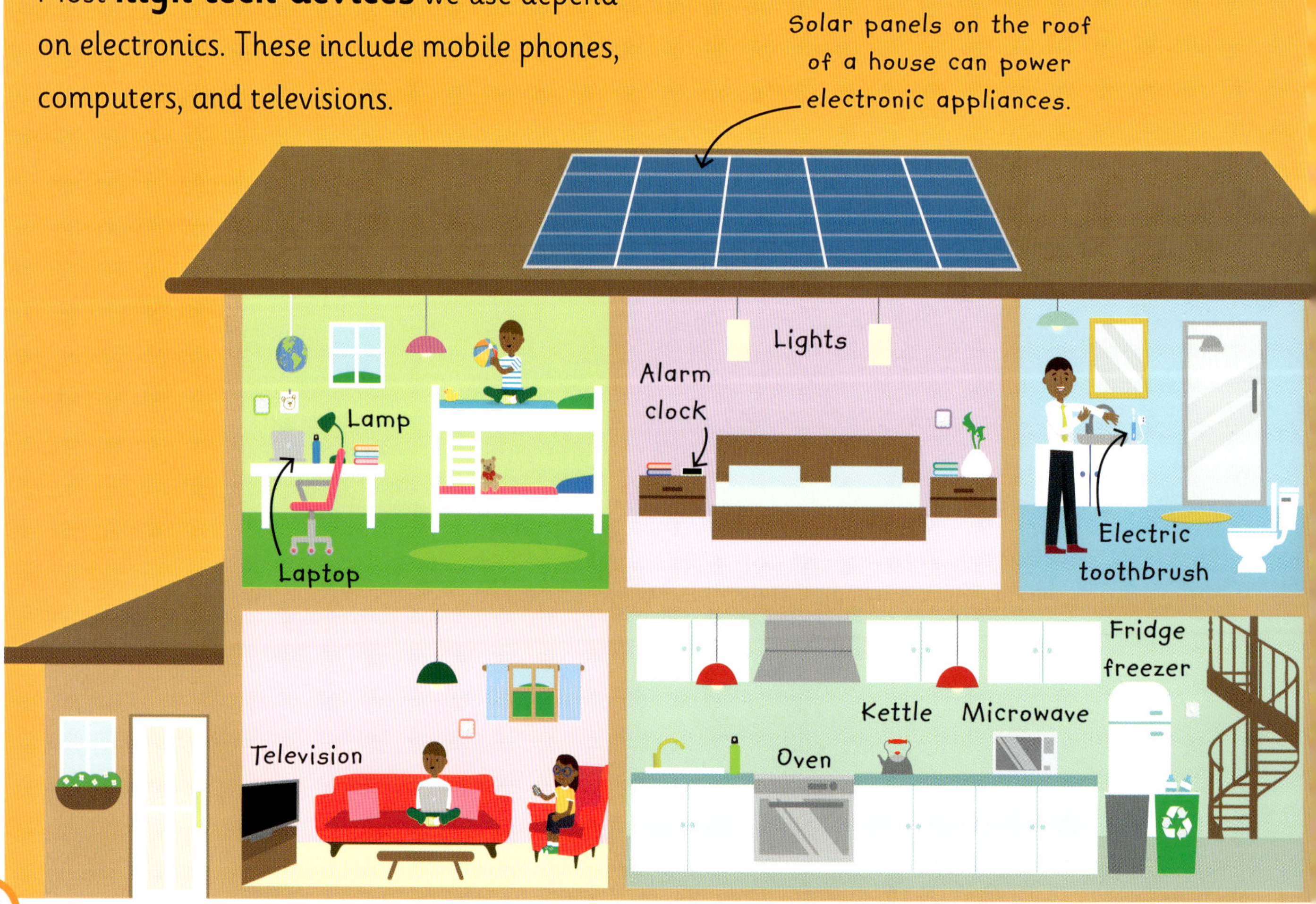

Solar panels on the roof of a house can power electronic appliances.

Lamp
Laptop
Lights
Alarm clock
Electric toothbrush
Television
Oven
Kettle
Microwave
Fridge freezer

Microchips

Electronic things often contain huge amounts of wires and switches. So that these don't take up lots of space, they are made into **miniature versions**, on parts called microchips.

A flow of electricity is called a current.

Special parts

There are many different parts in electronics, and each of them does a particular job. Here are a few examples:

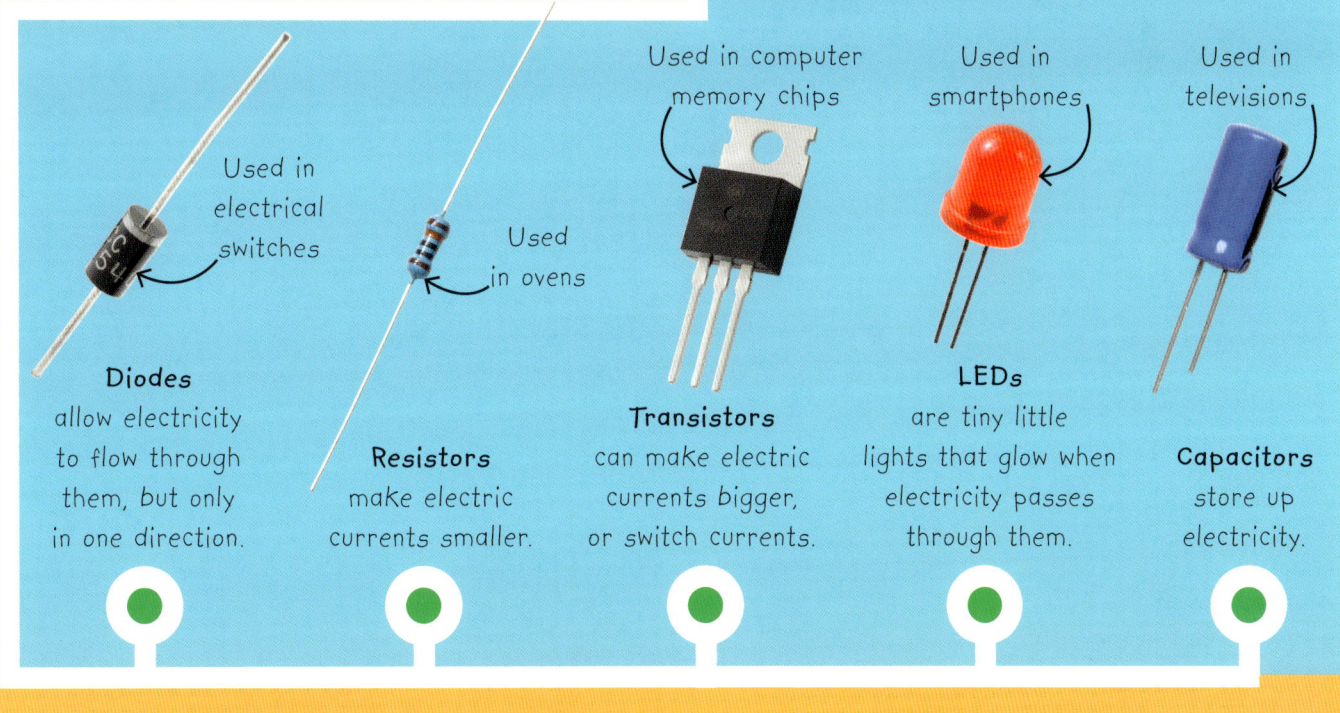

Diodes allow electricity to flow through them, but only in one direction. — Used in electrical switches

Resistors make electric currents smaller. — Used in ovens

Transistors can make electric currents bigger, or switch currents. — Used in computer memory chips

LEDs are tiny little lights that glow when electricity passes through them. — Used in smartphones

Capacitors store up electricity. — Used in televisions

Early computers were the size of rooms!

Radio and television

Turning on the radio or switching on the television offers an almost **endless choice** of music, news, entertainment, and film. But these two inventions only exist because of ingenious thought and incredible design.

Marconi's wireless telegraph

Radio waves

In 1901, Italian inventor Guglielmo Marconi's telegraph sent **invisible** radio waves across the Atlantic Ocean **without cables or wires**. In 1906, the first voice was heard over the radio.

How it works

Radio uses a **transmitter** and a **receiver**. The transmitter converts sound into radio waves and sends them out. The receiver detects the waves and converts them back into sound.

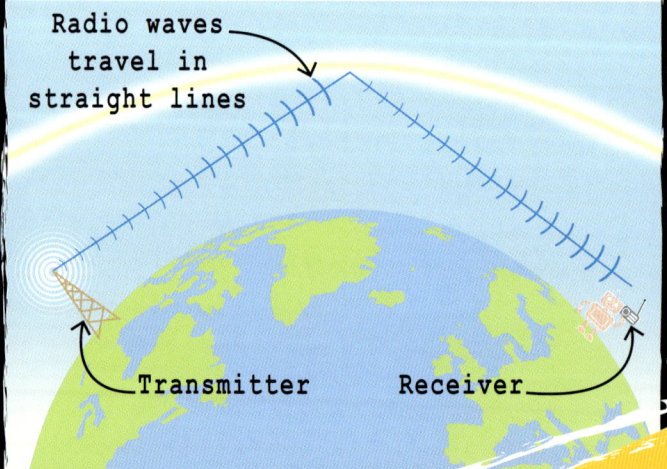

Radio waves travel in straight lines

Transmitter   Receiver

Radio waves are SO FAST they can travel SEVEN

150

Biscuit box

The first **television** was made by John Logie Baird using a tea chest, biscuit tins, hat boxes, and knitting needles! In 1928, he transmitted television across the Atlantic Ocean.

First working television

It's not REALLY a box of biscuits! Shame!

Smart TV

Televisions have grown smarter in the 21st century, with both an antenna and an **internet** connection. Images are clearer and viewers can **stream** their own music and videos and choose from thousands of films and programmes.

How it works

Cameras record programmes and send them out as **electrical waves**. Space satellites detect the radio waves and then they are picked up by satellite dishes on Earth and sent to the TV via a cable. The TV converts the waves back into images and sound.

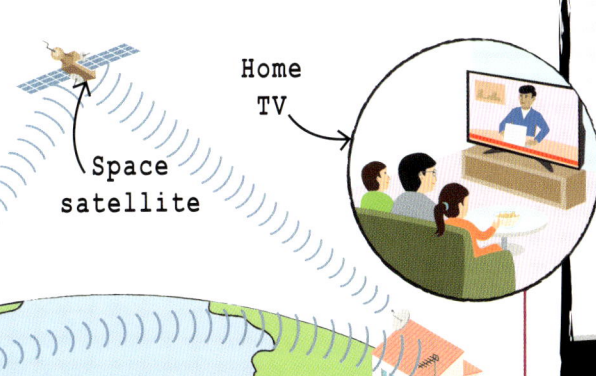

Broadcaster · Space satellite · Home TV

There are 1.7 BILLION televisions being watched around the world.

TIMES around the world in a second!

Computers

A computer is **a machine, with lots of tiny parts inside**. These parts allow the computer to follow our instructions, performing all sorts of different tasks.

How do they work?
Computers **follow our instructions**. We can give them information, they store information, and they can give us information.

Mouse

Big and small
Computers come in a huge range of shapes and sizes. Desktops and laptops are computers, and so are **tablets, smartphones, and smartwatches**. On the bigger end of the scale are very powerful supercomputers, which can fill whole buildings.

Smartphone

Supercomputer

We can **store** files inside a computer, such as photos and documents.

Hard drive

When we ask a computer to do something, it **outputs** that thing. The information we have asked for can be given to us in a number of ways, for example on a monitor, speakers, or printer.

Keyboard

Chip

Monitor

Input devices let us tell a computer what we would like it to do. This could be with a microphone, mouse, or keyboard.

The electronics inside the computer are like its brains. They **process** everything, allowing the computer to perform its tasks.

Inside a computer

We are used to seeing computer screens, keyboards, and mice. But there is a lot more inside a computer, which is what **makes it work**.

The **motherboard** is a circuit that holds together all the computer's electronics.

RAM is the computer's short-term memory. It stores information only when the computer is working.

The **hard drive** is a different sort of memory, which stores information even when the computer is turned off.

Our world contains billions of computers!

The Internet

Computers all over the world are linked together by **a huge network** known as the Internet. It allows us to look things up, send each other messages, and go shopping, all at lightning speed.

How it works

Computers link all across the world, sending information, via servers.

Servers provide services, such as email, to a computer, known as a client.

Smartphone

Tablet

Desktop computer

Computers everywhere

It's not just desktop computers that can access the Internet – **smartphones and tablets** can too. They let us access the Internet from almost anywhere.

The Internet was invented in 1983.

The Internet is used by

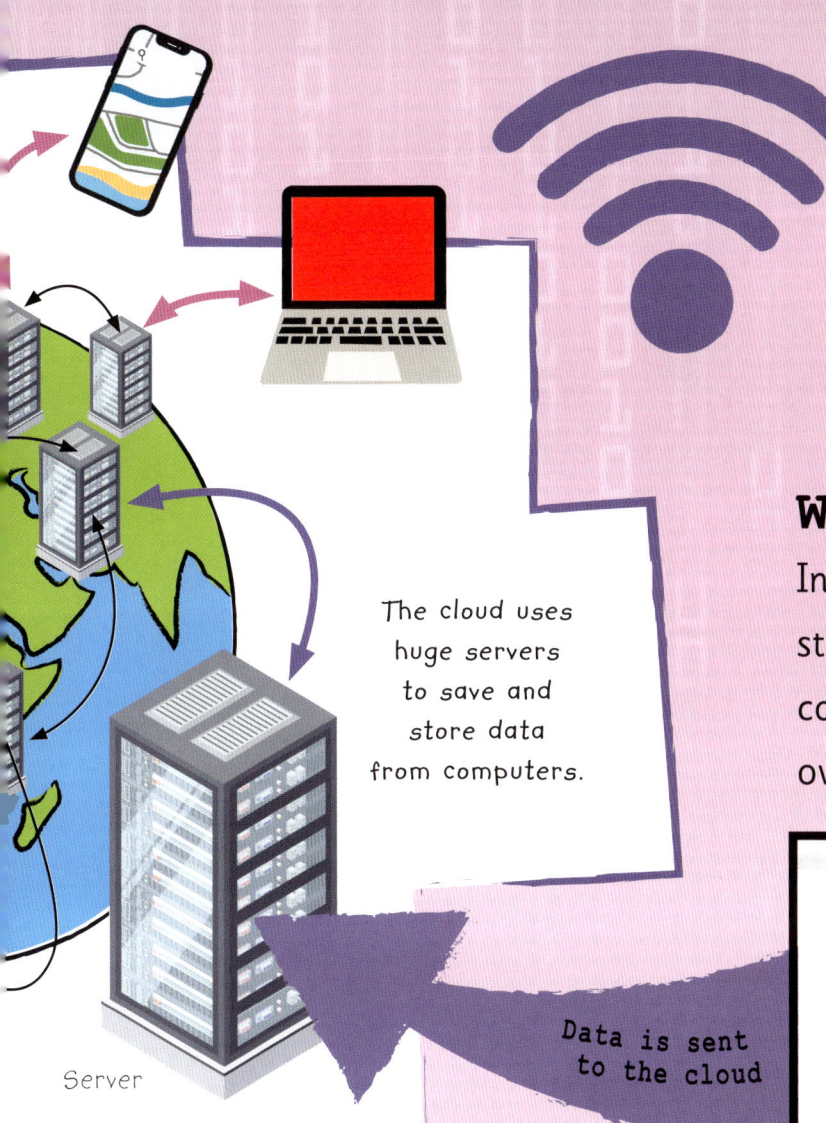

The cloud uses huge servers to save and store data from computers.

Data is sent to the cloud

Server

Wi-Fi

At first, you could only use the Internet if your computer was linked to it using wires. Today, we can link up using **radio waves**, or "Wi-Fi".

Websites

Information on the Internet is stored as websites. A website is a collection of pages, which has its own **unique address**, or URL.

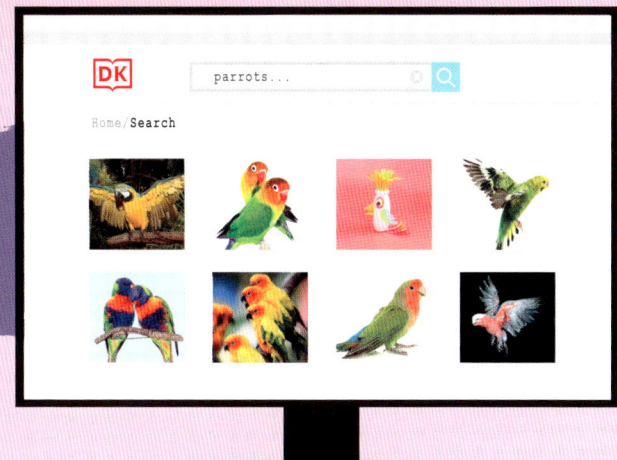

Website

Cloud storage

When we talk about computers, clouds have nothing to do with weather! A **cloud** is a way of storing your information **somewhere else**, rather than inside your computer.

The Internet on the move

more than 5 BILLION PEOPLE!

There are more than 10 million robots today. Biomimetic robots look and

Robots

The first robots were invented in the **1950s** as basic machines to perform routine and repetitive tasks. Since then, technology has developed so quickly that modern robots are now **super smart** and **busy at work** across lots of different businesses.

Robot means "forced work", which describes how robots are designed to carry out tasks automatically. Robots don't get tired, stop, or complain. They are quick and efficient, and can be designed to do repetitive tasks or heavy lifting.

A roboticist programs the computer in a robot to perform a specific task using a set of instructions. These commands are processed by the computer, and the task is completed by the robot's parts and machinery.

act like animals, including snakes, kangaroos, and dogs!

In action

Factory robots help in factories where they assemble cars and build parts without error.

Surgical robots can perform medical operations with great care and accuracy.

Space robots explore stars and planets, while scientists control them from Earth.

Chess robots can challenge chess world champions.

Amazing AI

Robots can be programmed with **artificial intelligence (AI)** to make them look and behave like people. Their advanced computer programs are designed to create robots that can have conversations, make decisions, tell jokes, and solve problems.

I am Sophia. I was invented in 2016, and am the first robot to have my own passport!

Never fear!

Some people are worried that robots might **take over the world**. However, even when robots look very realistic, they are still being controlled by humans.

Space

Look up at night and you might see some of the brightest stars twinkling in the dark. But out there in the deep, black sky, there are billions of others, along with **planets**, **asteroids**, our own **spaceships** — and many mysteries still to be discovered.

The Universe contains things we haven't found yet.

The Earth in the Solar System.

Earth
We live on a **planet** called Earth.

Our Solar System
Earth is one of eight planets that travel around the Sun, a **star**.

The Universe

Our planet is just a **tiny speck** in space. All around us is a vast expanse (region) known as the Universe.

The question of why space is dark is called the Olbers' Paradox.

Light years

Space is so huge that our usual measurements aren't very useful. Instead, we **measure space distances** in light years. Each light year is the distance light can travel in one year.

Scientists believe that the Universe began with the Big Bang. This is a moment when all the matter in the Universe that was squashed together into one place, expanded really quickly.

Our galaxy

The Sun is one of around 100 billion stars that make up our galaxy (group of stars). This is called the **Milky Way**.

The Solar System in the Milky Way.

The Universe

There are **billions of galaxies** in the Universe.

The Milky Way in the Universe.

The Solar System

Our Solar System is the group of planets and other objects around the Sun. There are **eight planets** and five smaller dwarf planets. All of them move constantly, spinning and orbiting (circling) around the Sun.

Mercury
Mercury is so close to the Sun that it is **scorchingly hot**. It has no air around it.

Mars
Red-coloured dust makes the surface of this planet an orange-reddish colour. It is the planet most similar to Earth.

Sun
The Sun is a star. It is huge, and everything else in our Solar System orbits around it.

Venus
This planet has a **layer of gas** around it that is so thick it is hard to land spacecraft here.

Earth
Our own planet! So far, it is the only place in space known to **have life**.

The SUN is not the only star that

Saturn
Huge rings of ice and rocky material loop around this planet.

Planets outside our Solar System are called exoplanets.

Is it a planet?
Dwarf planets are similar to planets. However, planets orbit around the Sun on their own path, without any space dust or rocks nearby. Dwarf planets, such as Pluto, share their path with other objects.

Pluto

Asteroid belt

Between Mars and Jupiter is a band of rocky objects called asteroids.

Uranus
Unlike all the other planets, Uranus **spins around** while tilted on its side.

Jupiter
This is the **largest planet** in the Solar System. It is so big that all the other planets could fit inside it.

Neptune
This is the furthest planet from the Sun. It is cold, dark and **very windy**.

has planets orbiting around it.

Rocky planets

There are four rocky worlds in our Solar System, including planet Earth. But **our home in space** is unique because it has all kinds of amazing life forms – including you!

Mercury's landscape has huge cliffs, deep ridges, and bumpy craters.

Volcanic lava covers most of the surface of Venus.

Mercury

Sunlight appears **11 times brighter** on Mercury's surface than on Earth, as it is so close to the Sun. It is the smallest planet and orbits the fastest. Mercury can be a scorching 430°C (800°F) in the day before plummeting to -180°C (-290°F) at night.

Venus

Almost as big as Earth, Venus has poisonous clouds and lots of volcanoes. It is the **hottest planet** of all, experiencing a temperature of 464°C (867°F). This means no spacecraft can get anywhere near it!

The smallest planet, Mercury, is 29 times smaller

Hard as rock

Each rocky planet has a solid surface made up of **layers of rock** covering a **metal core**. The rocky planets are smaller and move more slowly than the planets made of gas. They are also warmer because they are closer to the Sun.

Vast oceans of water have earned Earth the name "blue planet".

Steep volcanoes, deep canyons, and ice caps make up Mars's landscape.

Earth
The **biggest rocky planet** is ours! Earth's closeness to the Sun means it has the perfect conditions for liquid water, essential for life. Two-thirds of the surface of Earth is ocean. Earth's orbit around the Sun takes 365 days.

Mars
Mars, known as the "red planet", is about **half the size of Earth** and the furthest rocky planet from the Sun. Scientists believe that water once flowed on Mars, so early forms of life might have existed here.

around its middle than the biggest planet Jupiter.

Gas giants

Half of the planets in our Solar System are **enormous balls** of **swirling gas**. If you stepped on any of them, you'd fall straight through!

More than 1,300 Earths could fit comfortably inside Jupiter.

It's a gas!
Four of the eight planets are gas giants: Jupiter, Saturn, Uranus, and Neptune. They are made up mostly of **hydrogen** and **helium gas**, with a rocky core in the centre. The gas giants are furthest from the Sun and each one has rings around it and lots of moons.

Jupiter
The largest planet has at least **twice the total material** of all the other planets in the Solar System combined. Jupiter spins twice as fast as Earth, and has 95 moons.

A violent storm on Jupiter, known as the Great Red Spot, has been going on for 300 years!

Saturn

Picture a planet hula-hooping! This is Saturn, the second-largest planet, with its great ring around the middle. Although it looks like one ring, it is actually hundreds of rings made up of **rock, dust, and ice**. Saturn has 146 moons that orbit the planet.

An area of thunderstorms on Saturn is called Storm Alley.

All the Solar System planets spin upright except Uranus, which is tilted at an angle of almost 98°.

Uranus

This icy planet is four times bigger than Earth, with average temperatures of −220°C (−364°F). Methane gas gives Uranus its striking blue colour. There are **28 known moons circling Uranus**, and Titania is the largest, measuring about half the size of Earth's moon.

Uranus has a smooth surface with no obvious features at all.

Winds whip around Neptune at 2,000 kph (1,200 mph).

Neptune

As the furthest planet from the Sun, Neptune has **freezing cold temperatures** and **raging winds**. This is the only planet in the Solar System too distant to be seen with the naked eye. It has at least 14 moons, and Triton is the biggest one.

Earth

Our planet is a very **special place**! Most of its surface is covered with an amazing substance that helps create life – liquid water.

Around the Sun
Earth isn't still. It is always moving, making constant loops around the Sun. This path around the Sun is called **Earth's orbit**.

The Sun

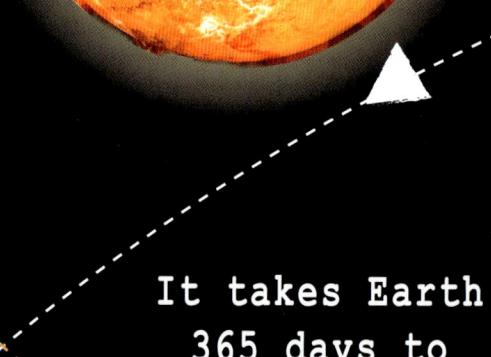

It takes Earth 365 days to orbit the Sun.

The Moon's orbit
Earth orbits the Sun, and is orbited itself, by the Moon. It takes the Moon around **27 days** to complete its orbit around Earth.

The Moon

More than a MILLION EARTHS

Under the crust

The inside of Earth is divided into layers.

The **crust** is the only part of Earth we can see. It is hard and rocky.

The **upper mantle** has hot rock, which can move slowly, like a thick liquid.

The **lower mantle** is hot, solid rock.

The **outer core** is hot liquid metal.

The **inner core** is hot, solid metal.

Weather

Earth is wrapped in a blanket of gases, called the **atmosphere**. Wind and water droplets move around in the lower parts of the atmosphere, creating our weather.

Life on Earth

So far, Earth is the **only place in space** where we know that life exists. All the life here depends on our most precious resource: liquid water.

The Earth

could fit inside the Sun!

The Moon

Our Moon is a hard **ball of rock** that moves in constant **circles around Earth**. It has no air or water.

 Full moon

 Half moon

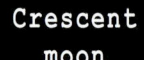 Crescent moon

The Moon is the only place

Rocky surface
The Moon's surface is **pitted with holes**, where meteors have crashed into it. There are also darker areas, which formed when **ancient lava cooled** into areas of rock.

Moon crater
Rocky area
Near side of the moon

Moon buggy

A steady view
The **Moon spins** as it moves around Earth, so we always see the same side – the near side. This photo of the other side, the **far side**, was taken by a spacecraft. The moon **rotates exactly once** in the time it takes to orbit Earth once.

Far side of the Moon

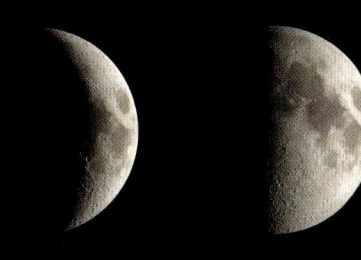

Phases of the Moon

Our view of the Moon in the night sky isn't always the same. The **shape of the Moon** appears to change, because different parts of it are **lit up by the Sun** at different times of the month.

New moon Crescent moon Half moon

in the Solar System that HUMANS HAVE VISITED - so far!

Moon lander

Earth as seen from the Moon

"That's one small step for man, one giant leap for mankind."

Footprint made on the Moon in 1969

Visiting the Moon

Humans have sent more than 100 spacecraft to the Moon. Most were robotic spacecraft, but some were controlled by **human crews**. Christina Koch will soon be the first woman on a moon mission.

Armstrong and Aldrin were the first people on the Moon, in 1969.

Neil Armstrong Michael Collins Buzz Aldrin

171

Space rocks

Space is home to all sorts of different types of **rocks**. They are organized into groups, based on what they are **made of** and how **they move**.

Asteroid

Asteroids
These rocks are **smaller than planets**, and move in circles around the Sun. If bits break off them and move towards Earth, they are given different names.

A smaller, broken off part of an asteroid is a meteoroid.

If a meteoroid reaches the air around Earth, it becomes a meteor.

When a meteor crashes into Earth's surface, it is a meteorite.

Impact!
It is very rare for meteorites to reach Earth. However, if they do, they can create **huge holes** in our planet, called impact craters.

The asteroid belt

There is an area between Mars and Jupiter that contains **millions of asteroids**. It is called the asteroid belt.

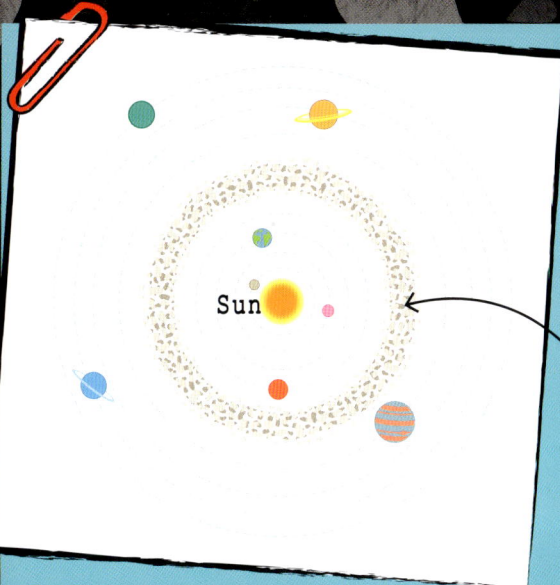

Asteroid belt

Some asteroids are big enough to have their own moons!

Comets

Comets are **frozen** balls of **ice and dust**. When they travel close to the Sun they form **tails**, which point away from the Sun.

Most comets move in huge loops around the Sun.

Dwarf planets

Pluto, Eris, Makemake, and Haumea are in the **kuiper belt**, a doughnut-shaped ring of icy objects that revolve around the Sun. Ceres is the only dwarf planet found in the **asteroid belt**.

Pluto

There are five known dwarf planets in our Solar System.

Twinkle, twinkle

Stars look like tiny specks twinkling at night. Really, they are **huge balls of gas** that are very bright and extremely hot. A star begins as a cloud of gas and dust that spins into a ball. All that spinning **makes it so hot** that the main gas, called hydrogen, turns into another gas, called helium. This is what makes the star shine. Stars eventually run out of fuel and die.

Red giant
When the **hydrogen** starts to run out, the star grows into a red giant star.

Blue stars are WARMER

Closest star
The closest star to Earth is **the Sun**. It gives us heat and light, which all living things need to survive.

In the sky
You can see thousands of **stars** in the sky. However, there are billions more that can be seen only with a telescope.

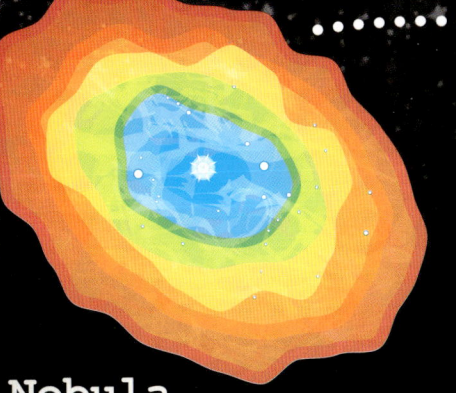

Nebula
Gas and **dust** leave the star, making a cloud called a nebula.

White dwarf
The core of the star that is left behind is small but **dense**.

One teaspoon of a white dwarf would weigh more than a pick-up truck!

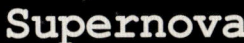

Supernova
Really **big stars** explode! These are called supernovas.

Black hole
Sometimes, a black hole is left behind. It **sucks in** anything that comes too close to it.

than yellow and red stars.

Proxima Centauri
After the Sun, the **next closest star** is Proxima Centauri. If you could drive there in a car, it would take about 50 million years!

Constellations
Some **groups of stars** seem to form pictures in the sky, called constellations. Explorers can use them to find their way.

Galaxies

Stars exist in huge groups called galaxies. There are **billions** of galaxies in the Universe of many different types.

Spiral
These galaxies look like they are spinning – and they are! Bright new stars form from **gas and dust**, usually along the arms.

Elliptical
These large galaxies form smooth, **round shapes** such as squashed circles, called ellipses. They mostly contain old stars.

Lenticular
These galaxies are a cross between spiral and elliptical galaxies. They have lots of stars **in the centre**, but don't have spiralling arms.

Irregular
These galaxies don't have a clear shape. They can be formed by two or more **galaxies crashing** into each other!

In the centre of our galaxy, there is a supermassive black hole, sucking in everything nearby. (Don't worry, we're a long, long way away...)

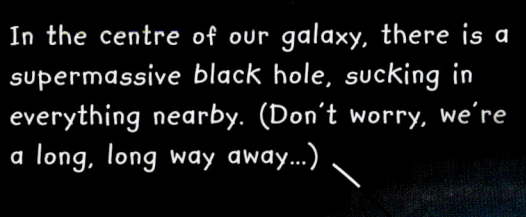

When you look up at night, all the stars you see are part of the Milky Way. If it's really dark, you might see so many that they make a milky band across the sky. You're looking out across the Milky Way!

Our planet, Earth, is just a tiny rock between two of the main arms of the Milky Way.

It is brightest in the middle because of all the stars there. They form a thick bar, between two arms.

Milky Way

We live in a **spiral galaxy** called the Milky Way. It is home to the Sun, the Solar System, and billions of other stars and planets.

The nearest large galaxy to the Milky Way is called Andromeda.

Space travel

For more than 60 years, space scientists have sent computers, robots, and **astronauts** up into space to explore.

Lift-off!

Rockets are extremely powerful. They have to be, to burst up into space carrying **astronauts** and **heavy equipment**.

Mission control

A team of people work at a **command centre**, known as "mission control", on Earth. They work to ensure all goes well with the space launch and flight.

NASA (National Aeronautics and Space Administration) controls its missions from the USA.

There are thousands of satellites orbiting Earth right now.

Satellites

Satellites fly around Earth doing **different jobs**. Some forecast the weather, some make phone calls work, and some help us watch TV.

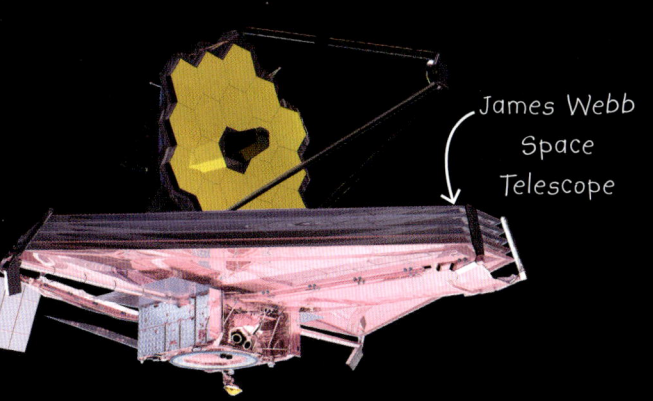

James Webb Space Telescope

Space telescopes

Telescopes on Earth have to see through dust and clouds to look into space. Space telescopes avoid the twinkling of the atmosphere which gives a clear view of **planets**, **stars**, and **galaxies**.

The International Space Station (ISS)

The ISS is the **largest space station** that has ever been built. Astronauts live and work in there. They do tests to discover more about how different things work and react in space.

Sometimes astronauts go on spacewalks outside, to build or repair parts of the ISS.

Astronauts float around inside the ISS.

Space junk

As more satellites are being launched, old ones stay in orbit. Space is becoming crowded. Scientists need to avoid crashing into space junk.

Life

You are **alive**, just like other **animals**, as well as **plants**, **mushrooms**, and tiny life forms, such as **mould** and **bacteria**. What do all these things have in common? Turn the pages to find out the remarkable **secrets of life**.

What is life?

Life first evolved on Earth about 3.7 billion years ago. Today there is **life all around us**, from the grass growing beneath our feet to the birds flying over our heads.

Same or different?
Living things vary greatly. They can be too minuscule to see, like **tiny** bacteria, or **mega-sized** and many times bigger than us, such as elephants. However, they all have some things in common.

Cells
All living things are made up of cells. These are the **building blocks for life**. Some contain one cell while others — like you — are made up of trillions!

Plant cells

Rabbits eat plants

Food
Living things must **eat to survive**. Plants make their own food, using sunlight, air, and water. Herbivores are animals that eat plants, while carnivores are animals that eat other animals. Omnivores eat plants and meat.

Growth

Living things grow and develop. Seeds turn into plants, kittens grow into cats, and human babies turn into full-grown adults. Most living things grow **bigger**, but some **transform** how they look, like a tadpole becoming a frog.

Kittens grow into cats

Movement

All living things can move. Some animals move at **high speed**, while others **go slowly**. Plants are fixed to the spot by their roots, but they still move by growing, stretching, and bending.

Snails move slowly

Cheetahs are fast

Reproduction

Living things can reproduce, or make other living things. Plants reproduce from **seeds**, while animals reproduce by laying **eggs** or giving birth to **babies**.

Dandelion seeds

Turtles lay eggs

Dolphins breath through their blowhole.

Breathing

Living things release energy from food. This is called **respiration**. Oxygen is usually needed for respiration, so many animals — including us — breathe in oxygen from the air.

Waste

It is important for living things to **remove waste** from their bodies. If waste builds up, it can cause illness and infection. The process of waste removal is called **excretion**. Many animals wee and poo their waste products away.

Poo is smelly!

Sensing

Living things use their senses to give them the information they need to find food and **stay safe**. Animals can see, hear, smell, taste, and touch. Plants react to sunlight, water, and touch.

183

The Kingdoms of life

Scientists divide the different types of life on Earth into groups, called kingdoms. There are **six kingdoms**, and each one gets bigger as more species are discovered.

Animals
This kingdom is the **biggest and best-known**, and includes birds, fish, mammals, amphibians, insects, and reptiles. Animals have many cells and can all move, grow, eat, and sense their surroundings.

Fungi
Fungi include everything from mushrooms and toadstools, to moulds, yeast, and lichen. They grow in **damp, dark** places and use decaying plants and animals for energy.

Plants
In the second-largest kingdom, the species vary from tiny flowers to towering trees. They have **many cells** and use sunlight to make food (photosynthesis). Most plants grow on land, although some live in the oceans.

In one meal, lions can eat a quarter of their body weight!

Some toadstools are poisonous, such as the fly agaric.

The animal kingdom has SPECIES, which is more

Life story

In the 18th century, Swedish scientist **Carl Linnaeus** began arranging living things into groups. His system featured two kingdoms – plants and animals – which we still include today among the six kingdoms.

Linnaeus named more than 10,000 life forms.

Bacteria
These microscopic, **single-celled** organisms live in any environment. They rarely cause a problem, but some can cause diseases.

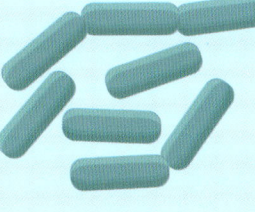

Trillions of bacteria are found almost everywhere you look.

Protists
Tiny single-celled life-forms that are not part of the animal, plant, or fungi kingdoms are protists. The protist kingdom includes **algae, slime, and mould**. They move around habitats, including oceans, lakes, and forests.

Algae is the main food of most fish.

Archaea
The most simple species exist in the archaea kingdom. They are basic single-celled organisms and **really tough**, living in the hottest or coldest climates or the most acidic or salty!

Archea were possibly the first forms of life.

at least ONE MILLION than any other kingdom.

Fossils

The past comes alive when we look at fossils. These are the remains of **prehistoric creatures** or plants that died a long time ago. They reveal stories of ancient life.

You could be the next child to discover a dinosaur. In 1811, Mary Anning was just 12 when she found the first ichthyosaur fossil.

Fossil hunters

Paleontologists are fossil experts who **study fossils** for clues about how a creature or plant lived. They use tools such as chisels to break into rock to carefully dig out fossils.

A Tyrannosaurus rex skeleton

Going extinct

Some living things have **died out altogether**, such as dinosaurs. When the last member of a species dies out the creature has gone extinct.

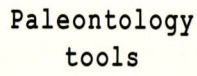

Paleontology tools

Forming fossils

Most fossils are formed in sedimentary rock at the bottom of the sea.

1 Layers of mud and sand cover the body. The soft animal parts rot away.

2 Over time, mud and sand turn to solid rock surrounding the skeleton.

3 Minerals in water pass through the rock into the bones. They become stone.

4 Earth's crust moves, and the fossil rises closer to the surface.

5 Wind, rain, or waves expose the fossil, which paleontologists dig out.

Fossil comes from the Latin word *fossilis*, which means "dug up".

Teeth

Fossil types

Fossils are usually the hard parts of an animal, such as the **bones or teeth**. Generally, the bigger the bones, the bigger the creature. The size and shape of teeth tell us what the animals ate. Fossilised footprints show the size of the creature and how it moved. Even fossilised dung has been found!

Feather

Footprint

Evolution

Living things adapt and react to changes around them. Evolution is the **altering of a species** over time, as the result of changes in the environment.

Tall tale
Some giraffes had longer necks than others and could reach the leaves on the highest branches. As they didn't have to compete with shorter animals for food, these giraffes survived.

Natural selection
Every animal or plant group has different characteristics. A big beak helps a bird eat larger seeds. A small beak helps a bird eat smaller seeds. If these random differences **help an animal or plant survive** and have offspring, then they will pass them on. Over time, only those with the features survive. This is called natural selection.

Darwin wondered if tortoises from South America reached the Galápagos Islands and then, over time, the species changed as some features were better suited to the islands.

Oceans to land
About **400 million years ago**, prehistoric marine life began to travel onto land. Some fish were struggling to survive in water as there were lots of predators and not much oxygen. The fish who could get oxygen from the air and lift themselves up on strong fins were more likely to survive. It is likely they evolved into the first vertebrate life on land.

Darwin's theory

English scientist Charles Darwin came up with the idea, or theory, of evolution. In 1831, he sailed to the Galápagos Islands off South America to study the plants and animals there. He realized that animals had **adaptations** (changes) that allowed them to make the best use of the food available.

Galápagos Islands

Charles Darwin

Noticing differences

Darwin thought that magnificient frigatebirds living on the Galápagos Islands wouldn't differ that much from their mainland counterparts. However, a study in 2010 suggests that the birds on the islands do have significant differences.

Birdie beaks

Darwin noticed the different finches living on the Galápagos Islands. Although they **looked the same** from a distance, they had beaks of different shapes and sizes. Those that had, by chance, hatched with a beak that was better at eating a certain food, survived better than those that hadn't.

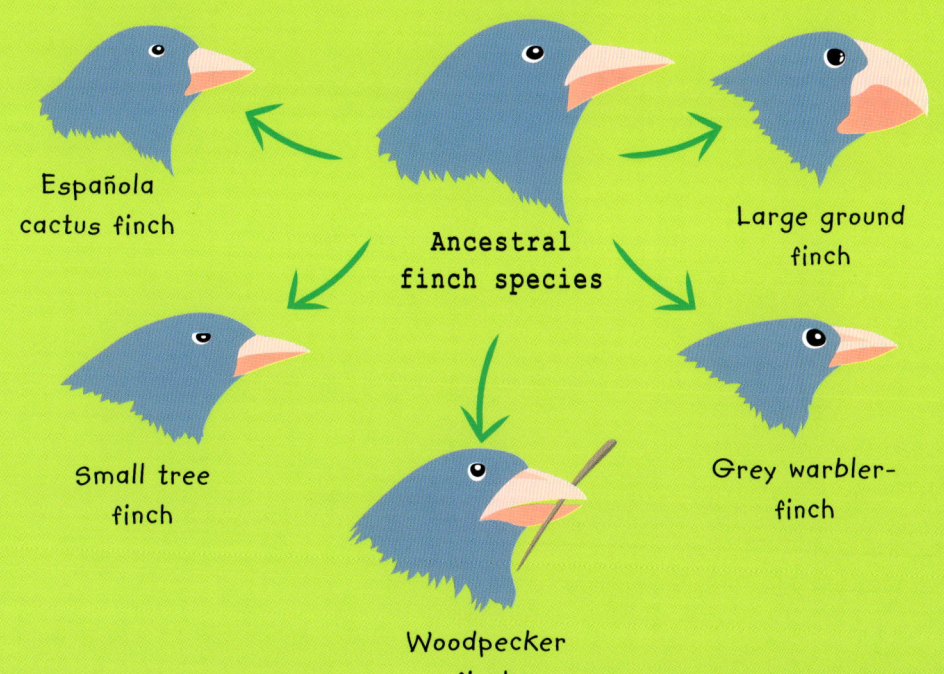

Española cactus finch

Ancestral finch species

Large ground finch

Small tree finch

Grey warbler-finch

Woodpecker finch

Magnificient frigatebird

Microscopic life

We are surrounded by microscopic life all the time. They are **too small to see**, so it's easy to forget about them, but they are inside and on our bodies, in the air, and in the water.

Close-up
Microorganisms are so small that they cannot be seen without using a microscope. **Microscopes magnify** the tiniest things to look bigger, so they can be studied properly.

Bacteria
Not all bacteria are bad. You have trillions of good bacteria living inside you that help digest food and **keep you healthy**.

The TOUGHEST microorganisms are tardigrades, eight-legged bugs that can survive without water or food for 30 years!

Dust mites
These microscopic creepy-crawlies live in the home, with one million living in your bed alone. Dust mites eat **dead skin flakes** that drop off your body.

Viruses
Viruses **invade the body** and use its cells to make more viruses. At least 200 different viruses can cause a cold.

Eyelash mites
These body bugs live in the hair follicles where eyelashes grow. They **clean us up** by eating dead skin cells.

Phytoplankton
The tiniest marine life are phytoplankton. They float along the ocean's surface and **turn sunlight into energy** to survive. There are too many phytoplankton to count!

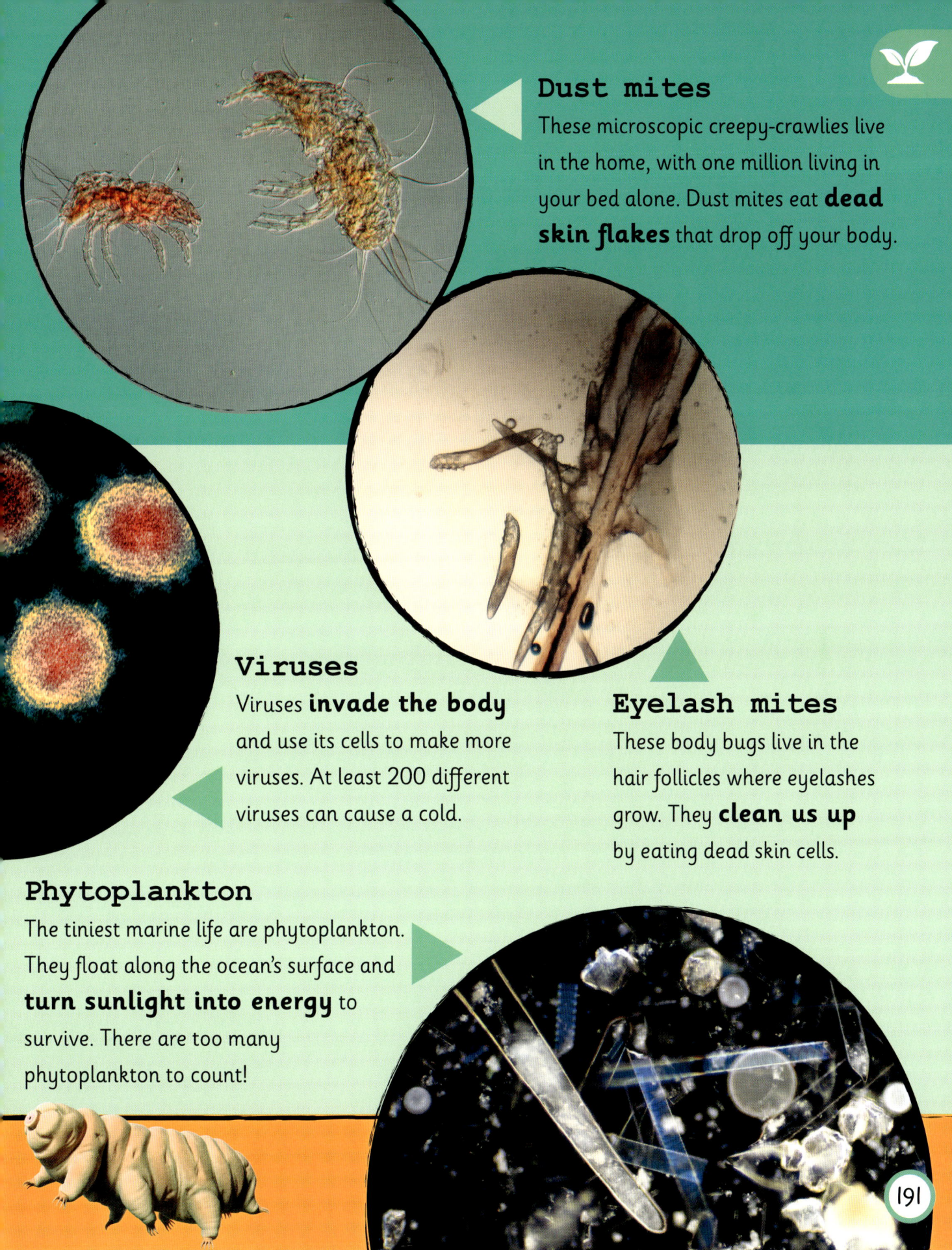

Cells

I need to be fit and flexible to get through through tiny blood vessels!

All living things consist of **microscopic building blocks**, called cells. Your body is made up of about 37 trillion cells, and they all have jobs to do to keep you working properly.

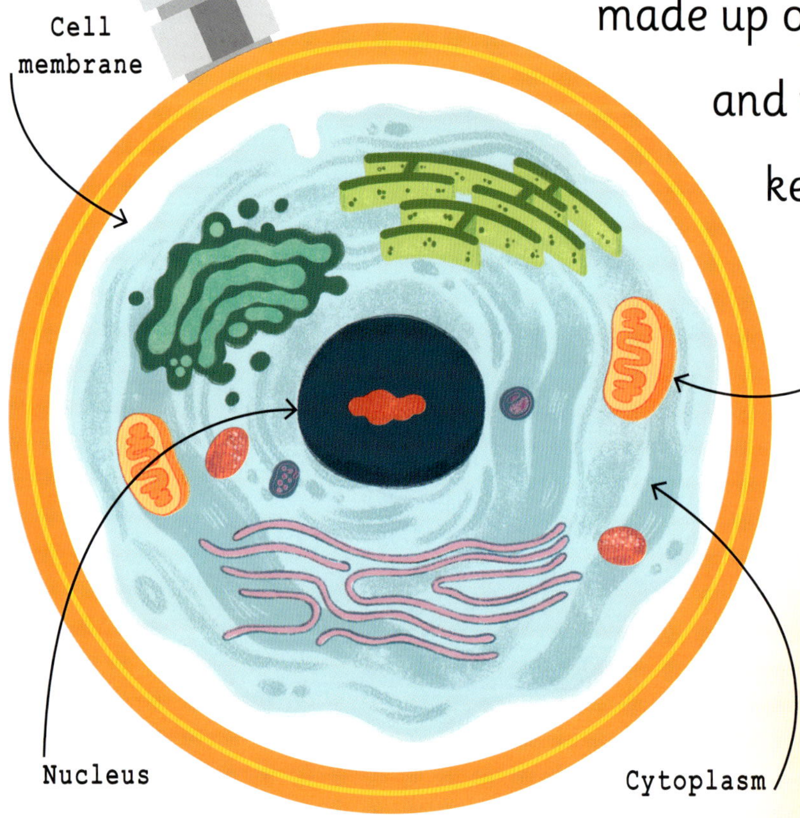

Cell membrane

Mitochondrion

Nucleus

Cytoplasm

Inside a cell

Every cell in the human body has the **same simple structure**. The nucleus controls everything. Hundreds of mitochondria release energy to keep the cell going. Cytoplasm is a jelly-like liquid that fills up the cell. The cell membrane that surrounds the cell protects it.

We white blood cells protect you from diseases.

A pinhead has room for about 10,000

Types of cell

There are about 200 different types of body cell, and each one has a specific role. They work together to keep the **body functioning**. Here are some of the most important cells busy at work inside you now:

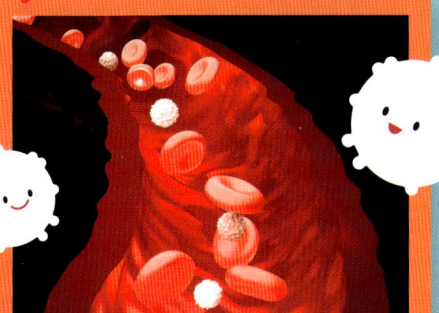

Red blood cells carry oxygen all around the cells of the body. Oxygen helps our cells release energy from food we eat.

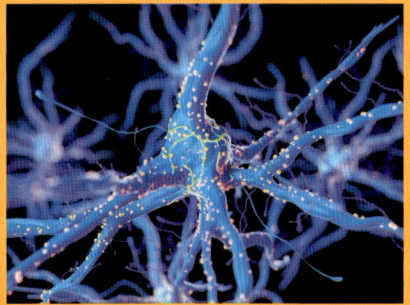

Nerve cells are the longest in the body. They send high-speed messages between the brain and the rest of the body.

Bone cells take care of bones inside the body. They can fix any bones that need repairing, and also make new bone.

Fat cells store body fat, which supplies the body with energy. A layer of fat can keep the body warm.

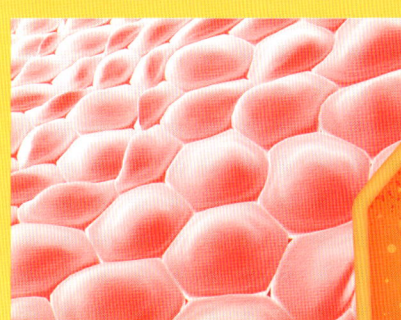

Skin cells make up skin that covers your body. You shed about 200 million skin cells every hour!

About 19 million skin cells would fit in a 20 pence piece.

Cells on a pinhead

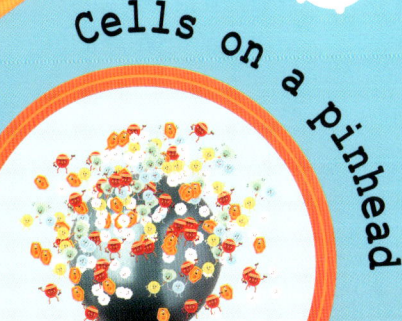

HUMAN CELLS on top!

193

Plants

We can't exist without plants. They produce the **oxygen** we need to breathe, and the **food** we need to eat. Fortunately, one-third of all the land on Earth is covered in plants!

Plant parts

All plants share the **same main parts**. They have strong stems to support them, deep roots to soak up water, and green leaves. Plants may also grow flowers or fruits, making food for hungry animals.

From tiny seeds

After a tomato seed is planted, its shell splits. Roots grow, then shoots sprout out. The plant flowers and its pollen is taken from one plant to another. The flowers turn into fruit. The fruit's seeds fall onto the ground and the process **begins again**.

Life cycle of a tomato plant

There are at least 390,000

Feeding themselves

Plants use sunlight, fresh air, and water to make food. This process is called **photosynthesis**. The plant uses the Sun's energy to turn water and carbon dioxide into oxygen and glucose (sugar). Oxygen goes back into the atmosphere.

Sunlight

Leaves soak up sunlight

Fresh air

Carbon dioxide

Oxygen

Plant transport

Each plant has its own transport network inside its stem, made of two types of tube. The **phloem** carries sugars made by the leaves to feed the rest of the plant. The **xylem** takes water and nutrients from the roots to share with the whole plant.

Plant sugars travel around the plant to feed it

NASA scientists grow lettuce and flowers on board the International Space Station.

Roots

Water

SPECIES of plant.

195

Flowers and seeds

Most plants **make more plants** using seeds. Flowers don't just look pretty – they are essential, because a plant's seeds form inside them.

Inside a flower

Seeds are produced when tiny **grains of pollen** from one flower reach another flower. The pollen is often carried by insects, such as bees.

The pollen from another flower must touch this sticky bit in the middle of a flower, called the stigma.

Pollen is made by these parts of the plant, which are called anthers.

Animals that carry pollen are called pollinators.

The seeds form here, in the ovary.

Different flowers

Flowers come in all **shapes and sizes**. Different insects pollinate different types of flowers!

 Rosette

 Dome

 Regular

 Bell-shaped

 Cone-shaped

Seeds can be dispersed by wind and water.

Coconut

These plants don't have scent or brightly coloured flowers, as they do not need to attract animals.

A flowering plant's life

Seedling • Adult plant with flowers

Making seeds allows plants to **make new plants**, over and over again!

New seeds

Growing seeds

To grow, a seed needs **water**, **soil**, and just **the right temperature**. Once it has those, it sprouts roots and then leaves.

Shoot starts to reach up through the soil

Shoot and first leaves emerge

Leaves unfold

Leaves start making food for the plant

Roots grow

Seed

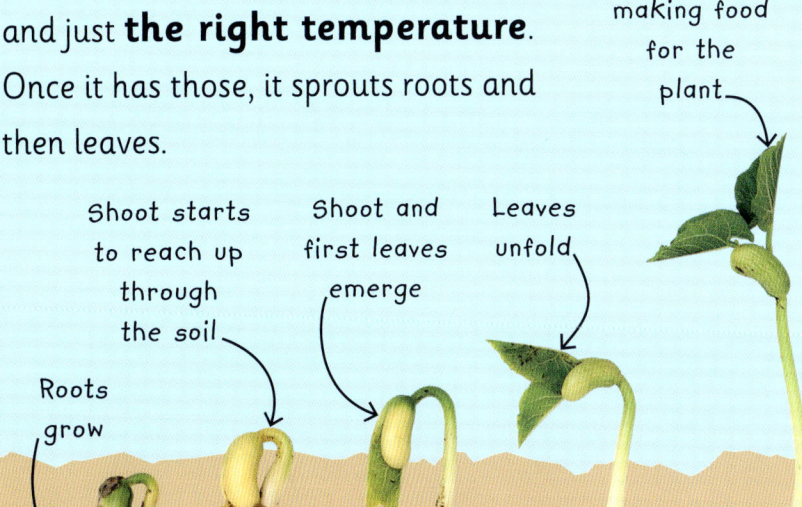

197

Soil

We don't always think about the ground beneath our feet. But it is a habitat full of nutrients, and home to to all kinds of **creatures and plants**.

Get digging

Have a little dig in the soil. It may look like a layer of dirt, but it is a **combination** of very important things. Although it's hard to get the exact amounts right because **all soil is different**, this pie chart shows the basic ingredients.

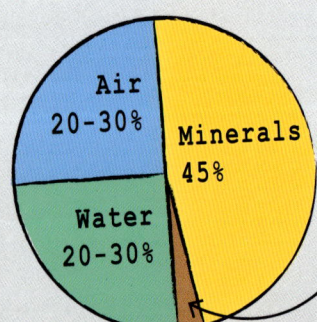

5% organic matter like plant parts, moss, manure, and poo!

Layered up

Soil is made up of several different layers, from the humus layer at the top to the bedrock layer **deep underground**.

Humus
consists of dead plants and animals that are slowly rotting away.

Topsoil
is where living things can be found, as well as lots of nutrients for plant roots to reach.

Subsoil
is full of clay and minerals that come from rock in the ground.

Weathered rock
is made up of pieces of broken rock that have come away from the bedrock below.

Bedrock
is the deepest layer of soil, which can be a variety of hard rocks, including limestone, granite, or basalt.

Types of soil

Sandy soil is light in colour with chunky grains that are dry to the touch.

Clay soil is darker and finer than sandy soil, and feels wet and sticky.

Water drains more quickly through chalky soil.

Growing up
Plants would topple over without soil for their **roots to grow in**. They stand tall and firm, spreading out their roots to **absorb water** and **nutrients** to grow healthy and strong.

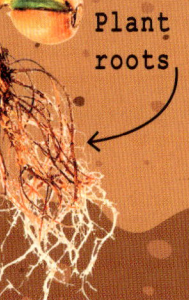
Plant roots

Stag beetle

Earthworm

Bug base
Countless creatures live in the soil. Take a look and you'll soon uncover wriggly **worms**, speedy **spiders**, and busy **beetles**. Soil provides shade from the Sun, darkness to hide away in, water to drink, and roots, fungi, and bacteria to munch on.

Soil allows us to grow the food necessary for our survival but it is being eroded (worn away) and destroyed at an alarming rate. Human actions, such as farming with lots of chemicals, are causing soil loss.

Fungi

Neither plant nor animal, fungi are basic living things that grow in **damp**, **dark places** almost everywhere on Earth. They are mostly underground, so only their tops can be seen. They include mushrooms, toadstools, and moulds.

A loaf of bread

Yeast is a fungus

Fabulous fungi

You may know fungi as the mushrooms you eat in a meal or the spotted red toadstools common in fairy tales. But fungi have other uses, too. They **break down and recycle** dead and rotting matter. They are also used to make bread, and feature in medicines, such as antibiotics.

Spreading out

Each single fungus has an underground network of root-like structures called mycelium. The part we can see is the fruiting body. This produces **spores** that are carried on the wind and **spread around**, so more fungi can grow.

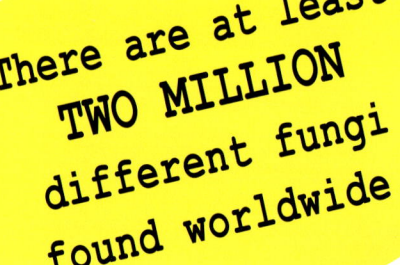

There are at least TWO MILLION different fungi found worldwide.

Hungry fungi

Like all living things, fungi need food to survive. They **absorb nutrients** from either dead or living plants or animals. Some fungi grow near particular plants so they can give the plants food in exchange for plant sugars.

The saffron milkcap often grows around pine trees.

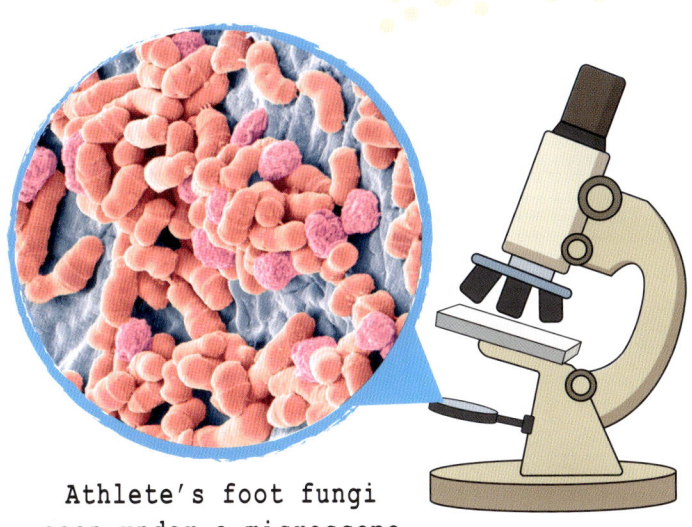

Athlete's foot fungi seen under a microscope

Wood Wide Web

We can't see it, but an **underground network** of fungi links tree roots and plant stems together. This is called the Wood Wide Web, and it is a vital part of the forest ecosystem. Here, food and nutrients are shared to ensure the forest thrives.

Flesh fungi

Some fungi can grow inside you without causing a problem. Others can **become an infection** and need treatment from a doctor. After playing sport, sweaty feet can provide a hotbed for fungi, resulting in an itchy infection called athlete's foot.

Warning!

Never eat mushrooms in the wild as some are very dangerous. The death cap is the cause of 90 per cent of deaths from mushroom poisoning.

What is an animal?

Welcome to the **animal kingdom**! From tiny ants scurrying along to jumbo elephants that make the ground shake, animals come in a range of shapes and sizes. But they have things in common.

3% are vertebrates.

97% of animals are invertebrates

Staying alive
Oxygen is essential for animals to survive. Some creatures breathe air to take in oxygen. Others, such as earthworms, absorb oxygen through their skin. Some marine creatures have gills that absorb oxygen from water.

Which animals are bony?
Most animals are **invertebrates**, which means they do not have a bony skeleton or a backbone. The rest are **vertebrates**, meaning animals with a bony skeleton and backbone.

Earth is home to about 7.7 million

Dinner time

Some animals, such as lions, are meat-eating **carnivores** that hunt prey. Many animals, such as giraffes, are **herbivores** that munch on plants. Other animals are **omnivores**, which eat both animals and plants.

Making sense

Most animals have the same five senses as us that help them to **stay safe** and recognize signs of danger. Some, however, use echolocation, which is the ability to sense how far away an object is using echoes. Others find their way around using Earth's magnetic field.

On the move

Plants grow in the same spot, but **animals move**. They may walk on two legs, four legs, or hundreds. Some have no legs and slither or swim. Most winged animals can fly.

Speaking up

Animals **communicate** in different ways. Some are loud, like roaring lions. Bees dance to tell each other where the best nectar is, while chameleons change colour to reflect their moods.

Young ones

Mammals carry babies inside their bodies before giving birth to live young. **Birds, fish, and reptiles** lay eggs from which their offspring hatch.

DIFFERENT animal species.

Animal groups

There are more than a **million types** of weird and wonderful creatures – including you! Let's take a walk on the wild side to **find out more**…

Sharks are fish and have cold blood.

Grouped together

Scientists put animals into groups based on their shared **characteristics**. A characteristic shows us how one group is different from another. This makes it **easier to study** animals and understand how they are alike and how they are different. Animals fit into one of the following groups.

← Whale shark

I'm the world's biggest fish and can grow to almost 10m (32ft) long!

Fish

These skilled swimmers live in lakes, rivers, ponds, and oceans. Most have **fins** and **tails** that help them travel through water. They breathe through flaps, called **gills**. Most fish are covered in protective scales. There are about 32,000 types of fish.

Birds

All birds have **wings**, and most can fly. Birds that can't fly can swim or run. They all have feathers, which keep them warm and help them fly. Most female birds build nests where they **lay their eggs**. Baby birds hatch by breaking out of the egg shells. There are about 10,000 known types of birds.

Mammals

Most mammals, including us, **live on land**. This group has **fur** or hair covering their bodies for protection and warmth. Female mammals give birth to **babies** and make milk to feed them. There are more than 5,000 types of mammals.

Sea otter

We move through the water in the same way that flying birds fly through the sky.

Humboldt penguins

Amphibians

These creatures live on both **land** and **in water**. Most are born in water and move onto land for part of their lives. The females lay eggs that look like jelly! There are about 8,000 types of amphibians.

Frog and frogspawn

Insects

More than one million species of insects have been identified, but there are probably millions more. Insects have **six legs**, a body divided into **three sections**, and **two feelers** to touch, taste, feel, and smell. Some use other body parts to sense things.

Dragonflies can fly in any direction.

Reptiles

Most reptiles live on land, but some live in water. They have **dry skin** covered in scales or plates. Their temperature changes to match how hot or cold it is. Almost all reptiles **lay eggs**. There are at least 10,000 types.

Bearded dragon

Metamorphosis

Some animals are born in one form, but then **completely change** into another! This is called metamorphosis.

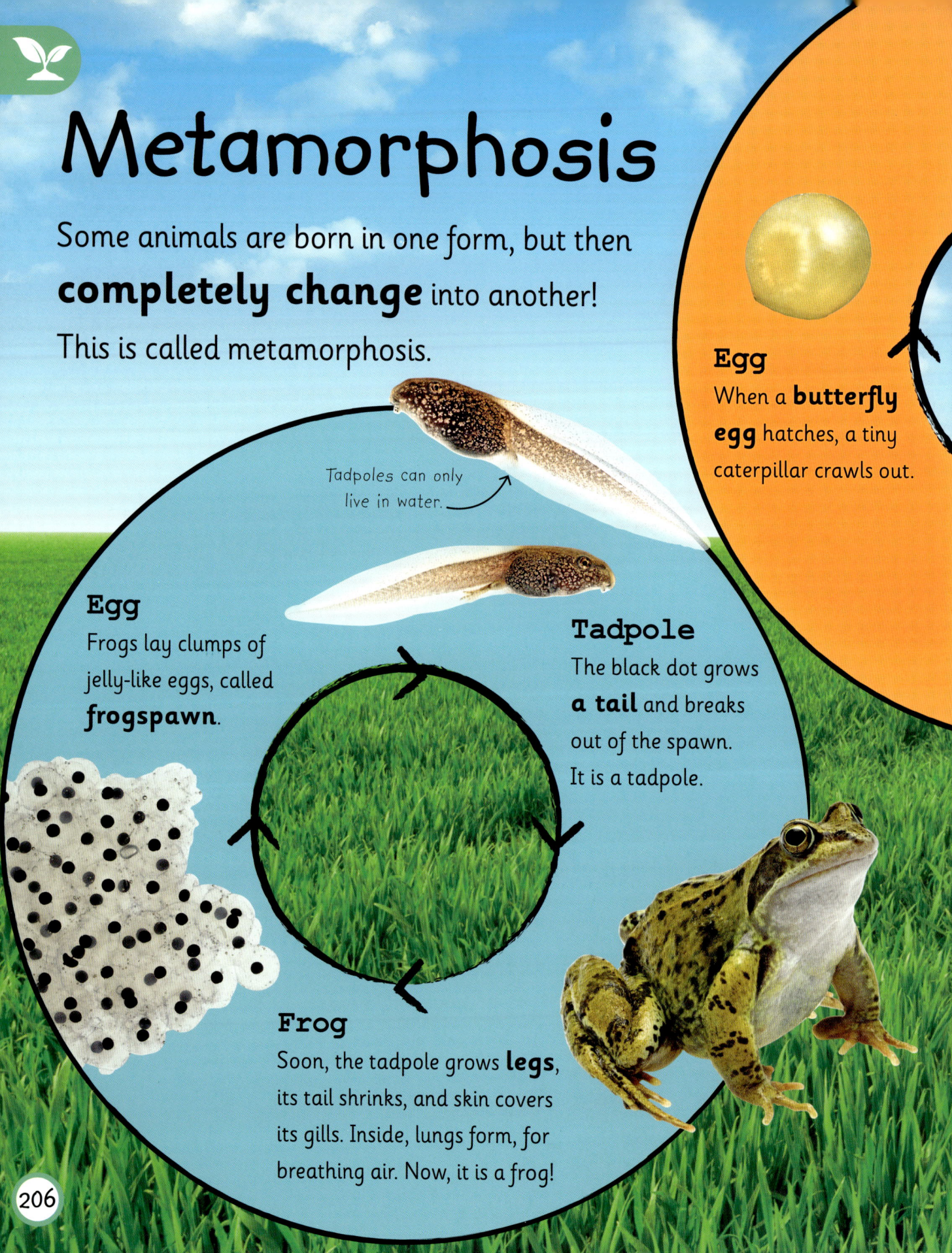

Egg
When a **butterfly egg** hatches, a tiny caterpillar crawls out.

Tadpoles can only live in water.

Tadpole
The black dot grows **a tail** and breaks out of the spawn. It is a tadpole.

Egg
Frogs lay clumps of jelly-like eggs, called **frogspawn**.

Frog
Soon, the tadpole grows **legs**, its tail shrinks, and skin covers its gills. Inside, lungs form, for breathing air. Now, it is a frog!

Caterpillar
The caterpillar grows, and makes itself a case called a **chrysalis**.

Butterfly
The caterpillar **changes** inside the chrysalis. When it breaks out, it is a butterfly!

"We get bigger as we get older. Imagine changing completely!"

Zoea
When a **crab egg** hatches, the tiny zoea inside swims out.

Megalopa
The zoea transforms into a megalopa, or **young crab**.

Crab
The megalopa takes a **few weeks** to become a fully grown crab.

Crabs have hard shells, which they have to shed many times as they grow. This is called moulting.

Habitats

Home, sweet home for plants and animals is called their habitat. This is the place **where they live** that provides them with all the food, water, shelter, and space they need to survive and thrive.

Tropical rainforests

Toucan

Hot rainforests experience regular **rainfall**, making them perfect homes for many animals. Trees and plants flourish here with both hot sun and heavy rain. Birds and monkeys nest in the trees, insects hide in the dense leaves, and jaguars roam the forest floor.

Most of the world's tropical rainforests are located in Africa, South America, and Southeast Asia.

Deserts

By day deserts can be **scorching hot**, so animals must find ways to keep cool. Some head underground or dig burrows. There is not much rainfall, so most animals get their water from the prey or plants they eat. The Sahara is the world's largest hot desert.

Polar regions

The frozen **Arctic** in the north and **Antarctica** in the south are known for **floating ice** and raging winds. Only the toughest plants and animals survive. Penguins, polar bears, and whales are covered in a fatty blubber that keeps them warm.

Penguins in the Antarctic

Coniferous forests

Evergreen trees in North American coniferous forests **don't drop their leaves** or needles in the autumn, so animals have foliage to hide from predators and sleep undisturbed. Grizzly bears go into a deep sleep, called hibernation, in dens dug into the ground. Owls emerge from the trees to hunt at dusk and dawn.

Mountains

Many mountain-dwellers, in places such as Asia, are covered in fur or thick feathers to **keep warm**. Ibex climb the tricky ridges. Birds of prey fly high, whilst white hares blend into the snow.

Ibex

Grasslands

Tropical grasslands have both **a dry and a rainy season**. Big cats hunt for food, while giraffes graze on grasses in Africa's tropical grassland (savannah). Temperate grasslands have hot summers, cold winters, and much less rainfall.

Giraffes on the savannah

Oceans

Oceans cover two-thirds of Earth's surface. From the sunlit surfaces to the darkest depths, there are all kinds of underwater ocean habitats. **Coral reefs**, in particular, offer plenty of food, warm waters, and rocky hideaways.

Food chains

Every living thing must eat or make its own food to survive. A food chain shows the **flow of energy** as plants and animals make or take what they need.

Linking up

Each link in a food chain is a plant or an animal. **Plants** are **producers**, while **animals** are **consumers**. Consumers rely on the producers that come before them in the food chain. If a species is removed from the chain, it can cause the consumer species that eats it to die out, too.

Predator

Predators are animals which eat other animals. This is an animal not hunted by anything else, such as a lion or a polar bear.

Consumer

In the food chain the consumers must find food or hunt prey. A lot of each producer species are needed to support a consumer species.

Producer

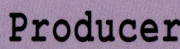

At the bottom of the food chain are producers. They are usually plants that make their own energy from the Sun and grow easily.

About 10 PER CENT of a producer's

All at sea

Here is an ocean food chain. The arrows show the flow of energy.

energy is passed to a consumer.

Endangered species

Many animals are **under threat** (endangered) because of what people are doing around the world. The numbers of these animals are falling, and they may be wiped out. There are people fighting to protect the planet and save the animals.

Melting ice

As people burn fossil fuels, to provide heat and run cars, the **planet gets hotter**. This makes the polar ice caps melt. Polar bears live on the ice and hunt seals that are resting on the ice. Without the ice they may not be unable to catch the seals. By using renewable energy, people help to fight global warming.

Deforestation

Forests are **chopped down** to make farmland or clear space for new buildings. This is called deforestation. Many forest creatures have to find new homes. To tackle this, trees are planted and some areas protected so they cannot be built on.

Save our planet

STOP NOW

Orangutan

Destroying rainforests destroys our habitat.

Save our forest

Ocean problems

Too much fishing reduces the numbers of ocean species, such as the Atlantic bluefin tuna. **Oil spills** from tankers and heavy boat traffic create pollution and endanger marine life. Marine Protected Areas (MPAs) are areas of the ocean where fishing and boating are carefully controlled to look after the animals living there.

HELP!

Close to extinction

When animals become very endangered with hardly any of them left, they may become extinct. This means the species is no longer in existence on Earth. Over the last 500 years, some **800 species have gone extinct**, including the dodo, quagga, and northern white rhinoceros.

Dodo

Dodos became extinct in 1681.

Hunting

Some animals are hunted by human **poachers**. An elephant may be hunted for its ivory tusks or a rhinoceros for its horn. The species can become endangered, and at risk of dying out. People try to stop this happening by banning hunting.

White rhinos have been hunted for their horns

Good news

Arabian oryx

There are some great stories of animals coming back from the brink of extinction. Zoos and sanctuaries can boost animal populations by introducing breeding programmes and releasing animals back into the wild. The Arabian oryx was facing extinction in the wild in the 1970s, but today there are more than 1,000 of them.

The human body

Your body is amazing. It can **think, breathe, jump,** and **poo**! But what's going on inside?

Organs
Some parts of the body, called organs, have **special jobs**.

Your brain tells the rest of your body what to do.

Skin is one big organ that covers your body and protects the things inside.

The lungs fill with air and then empty when you breathe.

The heart pumps blood around your body.

The liver cleans blood and keeps it healthy.

Your two kidneys help you get rid of waste, making urine (wee).

Blood
Blood flows around in pipes called **arteries** and **veins**. Every part of your body needs blood to make it work.

Red blood cells carry oxygen around the body.

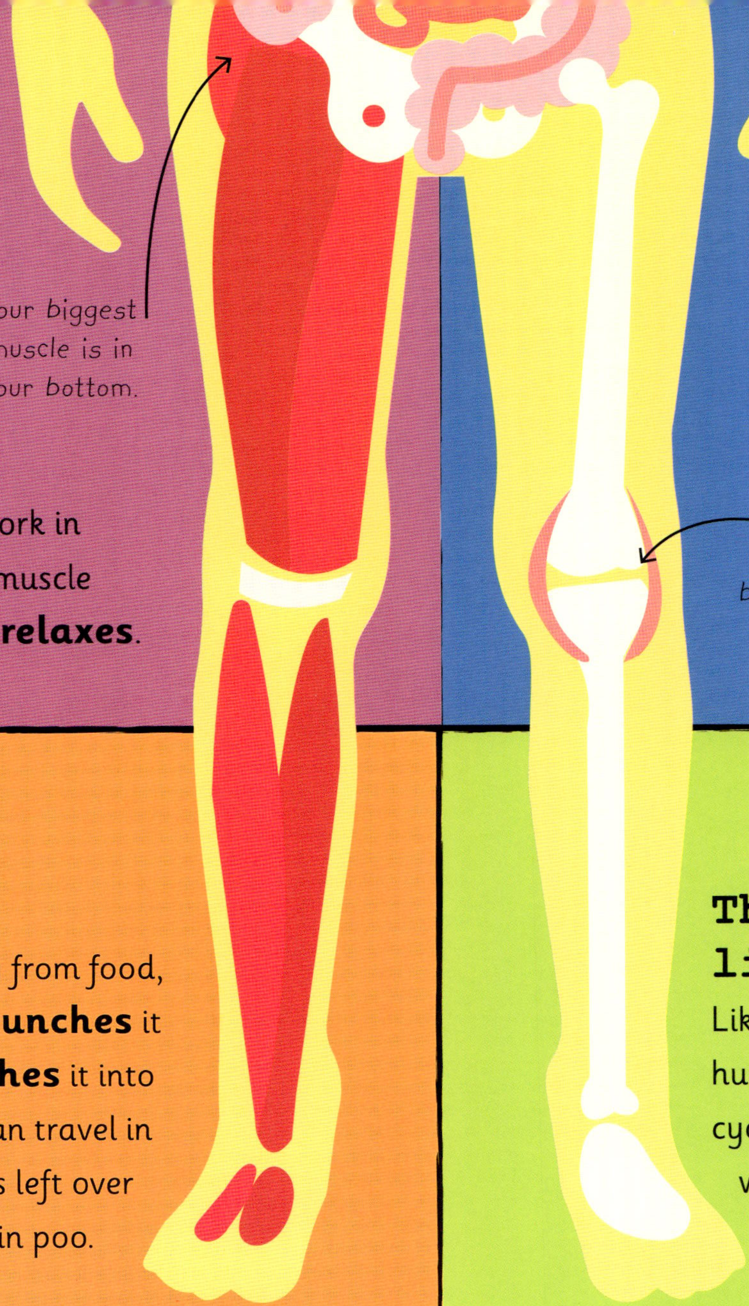

Bones

When you are born you have 270 bones. They fuse as you age. Adults have around 206 bones. Bones make up your **skeleton**.

Ligaments connect your bones together.

The human life cycle

Like all other animals, humans follow a life cycle. We are **born**, we **grow**, and we **die**.

Muscles

Meaty muscles work in pairs. When one muscle **pulls**, the other **relaxes**.

Your biggest muscle is in your bottom.

Poo

To get energy from food, your body **crunches** it up and **mushes** it into things that can travel in blood. What's left over it gets rid of, in poo.

Nutrition

Food contains substances called nutrients that you need to **live** and **grow**. Food can be split into important food groups.

Protein
Meat, **fish**, **eggs**, and **beans** are rich in protein, which helps muscles stay strong.

Dairy products
Food made from **milk** contains **calcium**, which is good for teeth and bones.

Fruit and vegetables
These foods contain many kinds of goodness, such as **vitamins** and **fibre**.

Carbohydrates
Bread, **pasta**, **rice**, and **potatoes** give you energy to do the things you want to do.

Your SENSE OF TASTE changes as you get older, so even

A balanced diet

To stay healthy, eat a mixture of things from **different food groups** every day. The more variety, the better!

Drinks, such as milk and fruit juice, give you energy and nutrients.

Future foods

Earth's population is growing, and it's difficult to feed everyone. Scientists think more people will **eat insects** in the future, as they provide protein in an environmentally friendly way.

Silkworm pupae powder

Silkworm pupae bread

if you don't like something now, you might later on.

Science words

This book is full of tricky terms used in science. If you're not sure what they mean, just look them up here.

Acid A chemical substance that can break things (such as foods and metals) down.

Atom The tiny particles that make up everything.

Cell One of the trillions of microscopic units that are the building blocks of living things.

Chemical reaction An event in which joined atoms break apart and rearrange into something new.

Combustion The process of burning.

Composite A material made from two or more things.

Compound A substance made by combining two or more different elements.

Conductor A substance that allows heat, sound, or electricity to pass through it easily.

Crystal A part of a mineral with a repeated pattern and a recognizable shape.

Density The amount of material inside an object and how compact it is.

Electricity A type of energy used to make machines work.

Element A substance that contains only one type of atom.

Energy A source of power to make things active.

Evolution The process in which living things change and develop naturally over time.

Fibre In textiles a fibre is a thin thread used to make clothing. Fibre in animal and plant tissue are cells that are longer than they are wide.

Force A push or pull that makes things start moving, move faster, change direction, slow down, or stop.

Fossil fuel A natural fuel that burns easily, for example, coal, natural gas, and oil.

Friction A force between two surfaces that acts in the opposite way to the movement, resisting that movement.

Fuel A material that is burned to create heat or power.

Galaxy   A huge group of stars, gas, and dust held together by gravity.

Gas   A state of matter with no fixed shape or volume that fills the space it is in.

Gravity   An invisible force that pulls everything towards the centre of the Earth (or any other body with mass).

Insulator   A material that does not allow heat, electricity, or sound to pass through it easily.

Liquid   A state of matter that flows – it takes the shape of its container.

Machine   Something that is powered by energy and is used to carry out a task.

Magnet   A piece of iron or other magnetic metal that powerfully attracts other objects containing iron (or another magnetic metal).

Mass   The amount of matter that makes up an object.

Material   A substance that can be used to make things.

Matter   The stuff that all things are made of.

Metal   A solid material, usually hard and shiny, that carries heat and electricity well.

Metamorphosis
The process by which some animals transform themselves into a very different form from when they are young to fully grown.

Mineral   A natural substance that grows mostly in crystal form, and can be polished to make gemstones.

Molecule   A group of atoms that are bonded together.

Motion   The process of moving from one place to another.

Nucleus   The central part of an atom or cell.

Oxygen   A gas in the atmosphere that supports life.

Particle   The smallest part of a solid, liquid, or gas.

Pollination
The transfer of pollen from one plant of a particular species to another plant of the same species.

Pressure   The force applied to something over a specific area.

Recycling   The process of using something old to make something new.

Renewable   A type of energy that won't ever run out.

Solid   A state of matter that holds its shape and volume.

Wavelength
The distance between the top of two waves.

Index

A
acids 38–9
air 13, 18, 36, 48, 52, 105, 113, 118
alkali metals 44
alkaline metals 45
aluminium 29, 42
amphibians 184, 205
animals 113, 116, 121, 184–5, 188–9, 202–13
archaea 185
argon 46
artificial intelligence (AI) 157
asteroids 172, 173
astronauts 178, 179
atoms 12, 13, 26, 29, 32, 34–5, 52, 105, 110, 114–15, 147

B
bacteria 74, 185, 190
Baird, John Logie 151
balanced forces 78–9
balloons 94
bases 38–9
batteries 132, 134, 140, 143
bending 88
Big Bang 161
birds 94, 189, 203, 205
black holes 175
blood 193, 214
bombs 115
bonds 15, 16, 104
bones 193, 215
breathing 183
brittle materials 10, 63
burning 11, 35
butterflies 206–7

C
carbohydrates 216
carbon 28, 32–3, 47, 52–3
carbon dioxide 19, 48, 49, 52, 53
cars 93, 143
cells 182, 192–3
centripetal force 82
ceramics 57, 62–3
chemical energy 104, 116
chemical reactions 34–5
chlorine 29, 47
circuits 134–5, 142, 143
circular forces 82–3
clay 57, 62–3
cloud storage 155
coal 12, 52, 53, 68, 144, 147
colloids 30
colour 121, 122–3
combustion 37, 92
comets 173
communication 203
composites 57, 66–7
compounds 32–3, 34–5
compression 19
computers 149, 152–5
conduction 11, 40, 112
convection 112
copper 40, 42
crabs 207
crystals 26–7
current 104, 107, 134, 135, 149

D
dairy products 216
Darwin, Charles 188, 189
decantation 31
decomposers 74–5
deforestation 212
density 98, 99
deserts 208
detritivores 74
diamonds 26–7, 52

dinosaurs 186–7
distillation 31
dust mites 191
dwarf planets 163, 173

E
Earth 15, 20, 22, 23, 26, 36, 50, 68–9, 86, 87, 139, 160, 162, 165, 168–9, 170
elastic 88–9, 107
electrical energy 104, 107
electricity 11, 33, 42, 45, 63, 93, 130–7, 142–9
electromagnets 140–1
electronics 148–9
elements 12, 28–9, 46, 52–3
endangered species 212–13
energy 69, 100–29, 146–7, 210, 211
engines 92–3, 117
evolution 188–9
extinction 213

F
fabrics 57
factories 70–1, 157
falling 107
fibreglass 67
fibres 64–5
filtration 31
fire 36–7, 110
fireworks 45
fish 188, 203, 204
floating 10, 98–9
flowers 196–7
flying 94–5
food 69, 103, 104–5, 147, 182, 194, 199, 216–17
food chains 210–11
forces 76–99, 138
forests 208, 209, 212

fossil fuels 53, 68, 69, 144, 146, 147, 212
fossils 186–7
freezing 20
friction 84–5
frogs 206
fruit 38, 216
fuel 36, 37, 143
fungi 74, 184, 200–1

G
galaxies 161, 176–7
gases 18–19, 20, 30, 46, 48–9, 50, 93, 112
gears 82–3
gems 23, 27
glass 57, 60–1
gold 12, 28, 29, 43
grasslands 209
gravity 86–7, 94
growth 183

H
habitats 208–9
halogens 47
hardness 11, 15
heat 33, 36, 37, 85, 102, 105, 106, 110–13
helicopters 95
helium 29, 46, 166, 174
human body 214–15
hydrogen 28, 32–3, 48–9, 166, 174

I
ice 20, 27, 50, 84, 212
igneous rock 23, 25
infrared 108, 111
insects 205
insulation 113
insulators 11, 46, 63, 134
International Space Station (ISS) 179
Internet 151, 154–5
iron 42–3, 139

J
Jupiter 163, 166

K
Kevlar 67
kinetic energy 105, 106–7, 117
kingdoms of life 184–5

L
land 69
landfill 73
lead 44
levers 90
life 180–217
lift 94, 95
light 102, 105, 120–9
light bulbs 117, 120, 133, 135, 142–3
light years 161
lightning 136, 137
Linnaeus, Carl 185
liquids 13, 16–17, 20, 21, 30, 31, 50, 112, 119

M
machines 90–1, 143
magnetic fields 138, 139
magnets 93, 130, 138–41
mammals 203, 205
Marconi, Guglielmo 150
Mars 162, 165
mass 87
materials 54–75
matter 8–53
melting 21
Mendeleev, Dmitri 28
Mercury 162, 164–5
metalloids 45
metals 40–5, 56, 72, 132, 138, 139, 165

metamorphic rock 23, 25
metamorphosis 206–7
meteorites 22–3, 172
microchips 149
microfibres 65
microscopic life 190–1
Milky Way 161, 177
minerals 11–15, 22–3
mirrors 124, 125, 129
mixtures 30–1, 32
Mohs scale 11, 15
molecules 13, 26, 32
Moon 87, 168, 170–1
moonbows 123
motion, laws of 80–1
mountains 209
movement 78–81, 92, 103, 105, 106–7, 183, 203
muscles 215

N
natural materials 56, 64
natural selection 188
nebula 175
neon 46
Neptune 163, 167
neutral ground 39
Newton, Isaac 80–1, 86, 122
nitrogen 18, 28, 48–9
noble gases 46
nonmetals 46–7
Northern Lights 139, 141
nuclear power 105, 114–15, 144, 147
nutrition 216–17

O
oceans 31, 51, 209, 213
oil 53, 58, 144, 147, 213
organs 214
Ørsted, Hans Christian 140
oxygen 18, 28, 29, 36, 37, 48–9, 194, 202

P

paper 68, 72
particles 15, 16, 18–19, 104, 136
periodic table 28
photosynthesis 195
phytoplankton 191
pivots 83
planes 94–5, 97
planets 162–9
plants 102, 103, 116, 184, 194–7, 199, 210
plasma 19
plasma balls 137
plastics 57, 58–9, 65, 72
polar regions 208
poles, magnetic 138, 139
pollen 196
potential energy 104, 106, 107, 117
power 69, 144–5
pressure 96–7
protein 216
pulleys 91
pushing and pulling forces 78, 79, 80

Q

quartz crystals 27

R

radiation 113
radio 150, 151
rain, acid 39
rainbows 120, 122
reactants 34–5
reaction 35, 81
recycling 59, 72–3
red giants 174
reflection 121, 122, 124–5
refraction 122, 123, 126–7, 129
renewable power 145, 146
reproduction 183
reptiles 203, 205

rhodium 41
robots 70–1, 156–7
rockets 93, 178
rocks 22–5, 41, 165, 172–3

S

satellites 151, 179
Saturn 163, 167
screws 91
sedimentary rock 22, 25
seeds 194, 196–7
senses 183, 203, 216–17
shadows 120
ships 98–9
sinking 10, 98–9
snowflakes 27
sodium 29, 33, 44
soil 198–9
solar power 145, 146, 148
Solar System 128, 160, 162–5, 173
solids 13, 14–15, 20, 30, 31, 50, 118
solutions 30
sound 105, 118–19
space 87, 118–19, 128, 129, 157, 158–79
spacecraft 63, 67
species 184, 194–5, 202–3, 212–13
stars 19, 174–5
static electricity 136–7
steel 43, 66, 139
storms 83, 145
stretching 89
submarines 97, 115
sulphur 47
the Sun 19, 21, 69, 87, 102, 103, 108, 110, 113, 116, 121, 122, 123, 146, 162–3, 168, 169, 174
supernova 175
suspensions 30
switches 135
synthetic fibres 64–5

T

tablets 132, 152, 154
tardigrades 190

teeth 38–9
telescopes 128–9, 174, 179
television 117, 133, 150
temperature 110–11
tidal power 145, 146
titanium 42
trains 92, 94, 141
turbines 93, 117
twisting 88
tyres 97

U

ultraviolet (UV) 108, 123
the Universe 160–1
upcycling 73
Uranus 163, 167

V

Van de Graaff generator 137
vegetables 216
Venus 162, 164
vibrations 118, 119
viruses 191
viscosity 17
volcanoes 24–5, 26

W

waste 183
water 13, 17, 20, 21, 31, 33, 39, 50–1, 69
waves 105, 108–9, 123, 150–1, 155
weather 169
websites 155
wedges 90
weight 87, 95, 99
wheels 91
white dwarves 175
white light 120, 122
Wi-Fi 155
wind 83, 133, 145, 146
wires 134, 142, 144
wood 56, 68
Wood Wide Web 201
wool 56, 64

Acknowledgements

DK would like to thank: Selina Wood for proofreading; Vanessa Bird for compiling the index. Rituraj Singh, Sakshi Saluja, Ridhima Sikka, and Samrajkumar S for picture research.

The publisher would like to thank the following for their kind permission to reproduce their photographs:

(Key: a=above; b=below/bottom; c=centre; f=far; l=left; r=right; t=top)

1 Dreamstime.com: Torian Dixon / Mrincredible (cra). **2 Dreamstime.com:** Nerthuz (tl). **3 Dreamstime.com:** Mykola Syvak (bl); Volodymyr Tsyba (cra). **Photolibrary:** Corbis (clb). **4 Dreamstime.com:** Ernest Akayeu (bl); Petovarga (bl/Factory); Ygcreativestudio (tr). **4-5 Dreamstime.com:** Chaoss (b/Road); Showvector (b). **5 Dreamstime.com:** Ominaesi (br/Building); Evgenii Naumov (br); Microvone (tr). **6 123RF.com:** lattesmile (br). **Dreamstime.com:** Markus Gann (tl); Tirrasa (bc). **7 Dreamstime.com:** Ovydyborets (bl). **Shutterstock.com:** Nanna71 (tr); Dima Zel (tl). **8-9 Dreamstime.com:** Bestbrk (Texture). **8 Dreamstime.com:** Wabeno (ca). **9 Dreamstime.com:** Oleh Muslimov (ca); Kelly Richardson (tc). **Getty Images / iStock:** mustafahacalaki (r); Vlastas (bc). **10 Alamy Stock Photo:** Art Directors & TRIP / Helene Rogers (bl); Superstock (crb). **Dreamstime.com:** Designua (tr). **10-11 Dorling Kindersley:** Colin Keates (b). **11 Alamy Stock Photo:** NASA Image Collection (cra). **Dorling Kindersley:** Natural History Museum, London / Tim Parmenter (crb). **Dreamstime.com:** Studiomixov (tl). **12 Dreamstime.com:** Kyoungil Jeon (bc). **12-13 Getty Images / iStock:** berya113 (background); mustafahacalaki (c). **14 Depositphotos Inc:** Brunohaver (cl). **Dreamstime.com:** Daniel Budiman (cra/Puppies); Chernetskaya (cra, c); Oleh Muslimov (cb); Vincent Giordano (bc). **Getty Images / iStock:** Vlastas (cb/Soccer ball). **Shutterstock.com:** Bamidor (tc); Kitthanes (cra/Photo frame); Tohid Hashemkhani (cr). **15 Depositphotos Inc:** Tanuha2001 (bl). **Dreamstime.com:** Mohamed El-Jaouhari (cr); Dmitrii Kiselev (cra); Pakhnyushchyy (Background). **Fotolia:** apttone (cra/Diamond). **Getty Images / iStock:** E+ / Andyd (c). **16 Dreamstime.com:** OSweetNature (bl). **Shutterstock.com:** ampFotoStudio. **17 Alamy Stock Photo:** Imaginechina Limited (br). **Dreamstime.com:** Aliaksandr Mazurkevich / Mazzzur (b/Texture); Shutterfree, Llc / R. Gino Santa Maria (tr); Grondin Franck Olivier (cra); Marazem (cr). **Shutterstock.com:** Somavarapu Madhavi (bc). **18 Shutterstock.com:** Yeti Studio (bl). **18-19 Dreamstime.com:** Alinamd (t). **19 123RF.com:** Zinkevych (cr). **NASA:** JPL-Caltech / UCLA (crb). **20 Alamy Stock Photo:** Martin Bailey (br). **Dreamstime.com:** Lequint (c); Ghm Meuffels (tl); Tartilastock (b). **21 Dreamstime.com:** Oleg Doroshin (cl); Sergey Novikov (tc). **Getty Images / iStock:** E+ / Peepo (br). **22 Dorling Kindersley:** Natural History Museum, London (bc). **Dreamstime.com:** Vlad3563 (br). **23 Dorling Kindersley:** Natural History Museum, London (crb). **Fotolia:** apttone (br/Diamond Jewel). **Getty Images / iStock:** VvoeVale (bc). **Science Photo Library:** Alfred Pasieka (clb). **25 Dreamstime.com:** Montree Nanta (ca); Pancaketom (cla). **26 Depositphotos Inc:** Jkirsch13 (bl). **Dreamstime.com:** Luchschen (br). **Fotolia:** apttone (bl/diamond jewelry). **Getty Images:** Jim Sugar (t). **27 123RF.com:** daboost (bl). **Alamy Stock Photo:** Jeremy Pembrey (cla); Maurice Savage (br). **Dorling Kindersley:** Holts Gems (c). **Getty Images / iStock:** OlgaMiltsova (tl). **Shutterstock.com:** Matt Ivanov (tr). **29 Depositphotos Inc:** Strelok (bc). **Dreamstime.com:** Melica (cb); Monkey Business Images (cr); Kelly Richardson (bl). **Getty Images / iStock:** E+ / StockPlanets (tl); Hidesy (ca). **Science Photo Library:** (clb). **30 Dreamstime.com:** Gresei (tr); Raja Rc (crb); R. Gino Santa Maria / Shutterfree, Llc (cr). **Science Photo Library:** (cb). **31 Dreamstime.com:** Shirophoto (tr). **32-33 Dreamstime.com:** Bestbrk. **33 Dorling Kindersley:** RGB Research Limited (tc). **Dreamstime.com:** Scanrail (c). **Getty Images / iStock:** vusta (tr/Salt). **Science Photo Library:** Turtle Rock Scientific / Science Source (tr). **34 Dreamstime.com:** Sjankauskas (bl). **35 123RF.com:** sergeypykhonin (tr). **Getty Images / iStock:** MediaProduction (cr); trenchcoates (ca). **37 Alamy Stock Photo:** Tommy (Louth) (clb). **Getty Images / iStock:** E+ / Pgiam (tr); TonyBaggett (b/Smoke). **38 Dreamstime.com:** Sommai Sommai (cr). **39 123RF.com:** stellar001 (tl). **Getty Images / iStock:** akinshin (c). **40-41 Dreamstime.com:** Meinzahn (c). **40 Dreamstime.com:** Ebo101 (br); Andrey Filipskiy (tl); Oceloti (tl/fire); Alexander Raths (cl); Gorg66 (cl/car); Chaiwut Sridara (tc); Yudesign (tc/bell). **41 Dreamstime.com:** Grecu Mihail Alin (fcl); Microvone (cl); Dzianis Davydau (cl/toaster); Nejron (tc); Olga Itina (ca); Lznogood (fcr); Yuriy Chaban (cr); Sergey Zavalnyuk (cb); Jatuporn79 (bc); Tomynurseta (crb); Misuhashistock (r). **Science Photo Library:** (cla). **42 123RF.com:** iarada (cr). **43 123RF.com:** Brian Kinney (tc); Aleksei Sysoev (cb). **Dreamstime.com:** Kyoungil Jeon (tl). **44 Dreamstime.com:** Joyce Vincent / J0yce (cb). **45 Dorling Kindersley:** Natural History Museum, London (cl, c); RGB Research Limited (fcl, cr). **Dreamstime.com:** Leung Cho Pan / Leungchopan (cb); Solarseven (tr); Olivier Le Queinec / Olivierl (br). **46 123RF.com:** Scanrail (bc). **Dreamstime.com:** Geografika (ftr, c); Wabeno (tr). **47 123RF.com:** leonello calvetti (b). **Dreamstime.com:** Geografika (cr); Teen00000 (fcra); Issaranupong Chaimongkol / Imooba (ca). **48-49 123RF.com:** Juri Samsonov (b). **49 123RF.com:** Kostic Dusan (tc). **Dreamstime.com:** (cb). **50-51 Dreamstime.com:** Radub85 (c); Ruslanchik (b). **51 Dreamstime.com:** Denys Bilytskyi (crb); Ludmilanaumova1985 (clb). **52 Dorling Kindersley:** Tim Parmenter / Natural History Museum, London (bl). **54 Alamy Stock Photo:** Dennis Campbell (br). **Dreamstime.com:** Chernetskaya (tr). **54-55 Dreamstime.com:** Nomadsoul1 (b). **55 123RF.com:** Violin / Tatiana Popova (tr). **Dorling Kindersley:** Gary Ombler / Steve Brown (bc). **Dreamstime.com:** Roncivil (br); Tirrasa (cla). **Getty Images / iStock:** Image_Source_ (ca). **Getty Images:** Ariel Skelley (tc). **Shutterstock.com:** Olly Kava (crb). **56 Dreamstime.com:** Jiri Hera (c). **57 Dorling Kindersley:** Gary Ombler / Steve Brown (bl). **Dreamstime.com:** Aliaksandr Mazurkevich / Mazzzur (cra); Larshallstrom (Background); Flas100 (notebook paper). **58 123RF.com:** tobi (Duck). **Dorling Kindersley:** Gary Ombler / Museum of Design in Plastics, Bournemouth Arts University, UK (bc). **Dreamstime.com:** Martin Green (fbl); Tirrasa (bc/Duck); Scanrail (cra); Yuliya Pauliukevich (br). **Getty Images / iStock:** Picsfive (bl). **59 Dreamstime.com:** 64samcorp (cra); Costasz (cb); Bidouze Stephane (c); Patrick Marcel Pelz (cr/recycling). **60 123RF.com:** grytsaj (tr); ruslan (tl/x2). **60-61 Alamy Stock Photo:** Wavebreak Media Premium / Wavebreakmedia Ltd UC31. **61 Dreamstime.com:** Arsgera (c); William Perry (br); Valentyn75 (ca); Aleksandr Kiriak (cl). **62 Dreamstime.com:** Doxtar (l); Roncivil (cr). **Shutterstock.com:** Olly Kava (cra). **63 Dreamstime.com:** Alvin Cadiz (c); Pavla Zakov (clb); Vitaliy Shabalin (tl); Chernetskaya (br). **Shutterstock.com:** schusterbauer.com (tr). **64 Alamy Stock Photo:** Riccardo Sala (bc). **Dreamstime.com:** Kbolbik (br); Ksena2009 (cl). **64-65 Dreamstime.com:** Timur Abramov (t). **65 Alamy Stock Photo:** dpa picture alliance / Antonio Cossio (bl). **Dreamstime.com:** Dmitrii Kiselev / Dimedrol68 (br); Zorandim (ca). **66-67 Dreamstime.com:** Belov1409 (c); Iulius Costache (Background); Smileus (b). **66 Alamy Stock Photo:** Dennis Campbell (bl). **Dreamstime.com:** Denis Dryashkin (tr). **67 Alamy Stock Photo:** Paul Heinrich (bc); Johner Images (tr). **NASA:** (ca). **68 Alamy Stock Photo:** inga spence (br). **Shutterstock.com:** Rob Crandall (tl). **69 Alamy Stock Photo:** America (cr). **Dreamstime.com:** Earnesttse (tl). **Shutterstock.com:** Peter Adams Photography (bc). **70-71 Dreamstime.com:** Misuhashistock (b). **70 Dreamstime.com:** Thossaphol Somsri (bc). **71 Alamy Stock Photo:** North Wind Picture Archives (cb). **Dreamstime.com:** Itsanan Sampuntarat (bl). **72 Dreamstime.com:** BY (t). **Getty Images / iStock:** Image Source (bc). **Getty Images:** Ariel Skelley (c). **73 Dreamstime.com:** Leklek73 (cb); Alfio Scisetti (cra); Travis Manley (cra/Bottle); Anton Starikov (tr). **Getty Images:** Karl Tapales (cl). **Shutterstock.com:** NataLT (cb/bag). **74-75 Dreamstime.com:** Michal Bednarek (t); Nomadsoul1 (b). **75 Alamy Stock Photo:** MSP Gardening Images (cla); Rachel Husband (crb). **76 Dreamstime.com:** Nagy-bagoly Ilona (br); Zerbor (cla). **76-77 Dreamstime.com:** Auris (b); Subbotina (br). **77 123RF.com:** Brian Kinney (tl). **Dreamstime.com:** Hery Siswanto (crb); Zerbor (cr, clb). **78-79 Dreamstime.com:** Aleutie (x5). **78 Dreamstime.com:** Steven Cukrov (cl); Ljupco (tr); Famveldman (tr/Child). **80 Alamy Stock Photo:** ART Collection (bl). **Dreamstime.com:** Pavol Stredansky (tr). **Shutterstock.com:** Creativa Images (crb). **81 Dreamstime.com:** Laudiseno (cr); Hery Siswanto (clb); Robertzsombori (c); Aldo Di Bari Murga (cb). **Getty Images / iStock:** DigitalVision Vectors / Jobalou (bl). **82 Alamy Stock Photo:** PA Images / Nick Potts (br). **Dreamstime.com:** Graphic Mall (cb). **83 Dreamstime.com:** Tomas Griger (tr); Irina Viatokha (bl). 84-85 **Dreamstime.com:** Klaus Rainer Krieger. **85 Dreamstime.com:** Raydignity (cla). **86-87 Dreamstime.com:** Dusan Kostic. **87 Getty Images / iStock:** Jupiterimages (crb). **Shutterstock.com:** Sashkin (br). **88 Dreamstime.com:** Anusorn62 (cl). **89 Dreamstime.com:** Nagy-bagoly Ilona (br); Alexey Poprotskiy (cl). **90 123RF.com:** Evgenii Naumov (bl). **Dreamstime.com:** Zerbor (tl, cra). **90-91 Dreamstime.com:** Auris (Grass); Subbotina (b). **91 123RF.com:** Erierika / Ilka Erika Szasz-Fabian (cla). **92 Alamy Stock Photo:** 2ebill (bl). **Dreamstime.com:** Vivellis (cb). **93 123RF.com:** Brian Kinney (tl). **Dreamstime.com:** Andrey Moisseyev (br); Zoom-zoom (t/sky). **Getty Images / iStock:** 3DSculptor (cr). **94 Getty Images / iStock:** Film Studio Aves (clb). **Photolibrary:** Corbis (crb). **94-95 Dreamstime.com:** Zoom-zoom. **95 Alamy Stock Photo:** LOC Photo (crb). **Dreamstime.com:** Tacettin Ulas / Photofactoryulas (clb). **96 Alamy Stock Photo:** RooM the Agency / Elizabethsalleebauer (cr). **Dreamstime.com:** George Tsartsianidis (tr); Marek Uliasz (bl). **97 Dreamstime.com:** Kornilovdream (tl); Mariia Petrova (tc); Volodymyrkrasyuk (tr); Viktoriya Kuzmenkova (br). **Shutterstock.com:** Muratart (cl). **98-99 123RF.com:** lattesmile (fishes). **Dreamstime.com:** Seadam (bc). **Shutterstock.com:** sumroeng chinnapan (t). **99 Dreamstime.com:** Archeophoto (br); Sven Hansche (tl); Tirrasa (cr); Dphiman (crb). **Shutterstock.com:** Keith Levit (c). **100 Shutterstock.com:** Blueee77 (bl); Can Yesil (cla); Dima Zel (clb); Prachaya Roekdeethaweesab (bc). **100-101 Shutterstock.com:** Pixssa (b). **101 Depositphotos Inc:** actionbleem (x5). **Dreamstime.com:** Wavebreakmedia Ltd (cr). **102-103 Depositphotos Inc:** Nik_Merkulov (b/Soil). **Dreamstime.com:** Iakov Kalinin (t); Nastasiasosedova (b); Rsooll (b/Background). **Shutterstock.com:** OleksiiShcherba. **103 Depositphotos Inc:** Krisrobin (crb). **Dreamstime.com:** Tamara Pechena (cb). **Shutterstock.com:** William Booth (cb); Ger Bosma Photos (c, cr). **104-105 Shutterstock.com:** Eric Wang (c). **104 Dreamstime.com:** William Berry (bc); Bakhauaddin Bek Sopybekov (tc); Viacheslav Krisanov (crb). **Shutterstock.com:** Can Yesil (cb). **105 Dreamstime.com:** Coolfinger (bc); Oleg Vorontsov (cla); Microvone (tr); Tigatelu (br). **106 Dreamstime.com:** Mazzzur / Aliaksandr Mazurkevich (crb); Yevgenij_D (cra); Wavebreakmedia Ltd (cr); Makidotvn (clb); Jy26 (clb/Background). **107 Dreamstime.**

com: Farek (crb); Anton Ignatenco (tr). **108-109 123RF.com:** Epicstockmedia (b/Wave). **Dreamstime.com:** Buddee Wiangngorn (b/Sand). **110 Dreamstime.com:** Guido Amrein (bc). **111 Depositphotos Inc:** Smuki (tr). **Dreamstime.com:** Juliengrondin (bc). **112 Dreamstime.com:** Carolyn Franks (crb); Rzoze19 (Background); Amir Magomedov (b). **113 Dreamstime.com:** Andreusk (Background); Alexey Sedov (tl); Alexander Ozerov (b). **114 Dreamstime.com:** Vasilis Ververidis (crb). **115 Alamy Stock Photo:** Magite Historic (br). **Dreamstime.com:** Tartilastock (tc, ca). **116-117 Depositphotos Inc:** Pakhnyushchyy (t). **Dreamstime.com:** Iulius Costache (b). **116 Dreamstime.com:** Anna Kraynova (bc); Sergejsolomatin (cla). **117 Depositphotos Inc:** Albachiaraa (cla). **118-119 Getty Images / iStock:** Roman Kulinskiy (b/Stars). **118 Alamy Stock Photo:** Blue Planet Archive AMD (bl). **Dreamstime.com:** Isselee (cl). **119 Dreamstime.com:** Kitchner Bain (bl). **Getty Images / iStock:** andy_Q (tc). **120-121 Depositphotos Inc:** Furian (prism). **121 Alamy Stock Photo:** David Chapman (bl). **Dreamstime.com:** Mbridger68 (tl). **122-123 Depositphotos Inc:** Pakhnyushchyy. **Shutterstock.com:** Pixssa (Rainbow). **122 Depositphotos Inc:** actionbleem (cb/x6). **Dreamstime.com:** Studiobarcelona (tl). **Shutterstock.com:** Prachaya Roekdeethaweesab (bl). **123 Dreamstime.com:** Peter Hermes Furian (cl); Влалй Барда (tl); Jeffrey Mills (cb). **124 Dreamstime.com:** Wabeno (tl). **124-125 Getty Images / iStock:** Natthanim (Background). **Science Photo Library:** Giphotostock (crb). **126 Dreamstime.com:** Nataliia Yankovets (c). **126-127 Alamy Stock Photo:** Rob Walls (c). **Dreamstime.com:** Aliaksandr Mazurkevich / Mazzzur (Background). **Getty Images / iStock:** Natrot. **127 Dreamstime.com:** Tetiana Shumbasova (br). **128 Dreamstime.com:** Mike Hollman (l); Mykola Syvak (bc). **129 Shutterstock.com:** Blueee77 (bc); Dima Zel (crb, br). **130 Dreamstime.com:** Punpleng (tl). **Getty Images:** Steffen Schnur (cb). **130-131 123RF.com:** Suti / Suto Norbert (br). **131 Dreamstime.com:** Chiradech Chotchuang (ca); Pixelrobot (tr). **132 Alamy Stock Photo:** imageBROKER.com GmbH & Co. KG / Ulrich Zillmann (br). **Dreamstime.com:** Ulkan120 (tc). **133 Alamy Stock Photo:** Panther Media GmbH / gmstockstudio (cb). **Dreamstime.com:** Shawn Hempel (crb); Pixelrobot (clb). **134-135 Dreamstime.com:** Yusuf Demirci (X3). **134 123RF.com:** Photopips (bl). **136 Dreamstime.com:** Aga / Agnieszka Mac Uchman. **137 Dreamstime.com:** Zimiri (tr). **138 Dreamstime.com:** Lucas Rozada (clb/Background); Joanne Zhe (c, cr, tr). **139 Dorling Kindersley:** Natural History Museum, London / Colin Keates (tc, tl). **Getty Images:** Steffen Schnur (br). **140 Dreamstime.com:** Bodik1992 (clb); Mikhail Kokhanchikov / Mik122 (c). **Science Photo Library:** Giphotostock (b). **141 Alamy Stock Photo:** Tom Walker (cra). **Dreamstime.com:** Yinan Zhang (br). **Getty Images / iStock:** Karl-Friedrich Hohl (cl). **142 Getty Images / iStock:** Thank you for your assistant (bl). **143 Dreamstime.com:** Damrong Rattanapong (tr); Takcrane3 (br). **144-145 Dreamstime.com:** Chaoss (c); Showvector (ca). **144 Dreamstime.com:** Ernest Akayeu (cla/Power station); Oleksandr Kyrylov (crb); Klaradohnalova (bc); Geografika (cb); Petovarga (cla); Pavlo I (bl, clb). **145 Dreamstime.com:** Ominaesi (cra); Microvone (crb); Orhidei (bc); Petovarga (clb); Punpleng (tr); Evgenii Naumov (cr). **146-147 Dreamstime.com:** Zoom-zoom (t). **149 123RF.com:** Samum (cb). **Dreamstime.com:** Tim@awe (crb); Korn Vitthayanukarun (tc); Vlabos (clb). **150 Dorling Kindersley:** The Science Museum / Clive Streeter (cl). **152 Alamy Stock Photo:** Everett Collection Historical (br). **152-153 123RF.com:** Petri Jauhiainen (Background); Maxim Basinski / Vasabii (ca). **153 Dreamstime.com:** Alexandr Kornienko (br); Suriya Yayubsuk (tc); Leung Cho Pan / Leungchopan (ca); Daniele Taurino / Sonica83 (cra/iMac Background). **Getty Images / iStock:** LyleGregg (cra). **Shutterstock.com:** NMStudio789 (bc). **154-155 123RF.com:** Suti / Suto Norbert (t/Background Texture). **Dreamstime.com:** Microvone (ca/Servers). **154 123RF.com:** Ramon Espelt Gorgozo / Ramonespelt (cb/Phone). **Dorling Kindersley:** Jamie Marshall / Jamie Marshall (cb). **Dreamstime.com:** Djahan / Vladimir Ovchinnikov (cr). **155 123RF.com:** Dmitry Pichugin (cb). **Dorling Kindersley:** Jungle Island / Steven Greaves (cb/Macaw parrot). **Dreamstime.com:** Abrosimovae (crb); PeterWaters (cb/Rainbow lorikeets); Kitchner Bain (cb/Sun Conures); Slowmotiongli (crb/Cacatoes). **Getty Images / iStock:** Antagain (crb/Budgerigar); Cynoclub (crb/Lovebird). **157 Alamy Stock Photo:** Westend61 GmbH / Anna Huber (clb). **Dreamstime.com:** Chiradech Chotchuang (br); Kittipong Jirasukhanont (tr); Sompong Sriphet (tl). **158-159 Dreamstime.com:** Torian Dixon / Mrincredible (ca); Wisconsinart (b). **159 123RF.com:** leonello calvetti (cra). 160-161 **NASA:** JPL-Caltech (c). **160 123RF.com:** leonello calvetti (tl). **161 NASA and The Hubble Heritage Team (AURA/STScI):** ESA, H. Teplitz and M. Rafelski (IPAC / Caltech), A. Koekemoer (STScI), R. Windhorst (Arizona State University), and Z. Levay (STScI) (br). **162-163 Getty Images / iStock:** Roman Kulinskiy (Stars). **163 NASA:** APL / Johns Hopkins University (cra). **164 Dreamstime.com:** Grejak (cl); Alexandr Yurtchenko (cr). **164-165 ESA / Hubble:** NASA, ESA and Jesús Maíz Apellániz (Instituto de Astrofísica de Andalucía, Spain)/http://creativecommons.org/licenses/by/3.0. **165 123RF.com:** leonello calvetti (cl). **Dreamstime.com:** Archangel80889 (cr). **166-167 Dreamstime.com:** Torian Dixon / Mrincredible (tc). **166 Dreamstime.com:** Nerthuz (crb). **167 Dreamstime.com:** Torian Dixon / Mrincredible (bl, crb). **168 123RF.com:** leonello calvetti (bl). **Dorling Kindersley:** NASA (cb). **Dreamstime.com:** Markus Gann (tr, clb). **170-171 Dreamstime.com:** Delstudio (t); Wisconsinart (Background). **170 Dreamstime.com:** Claudio Caridi (br). **Shutterstock.com:** Nanna71 (cl). **171 Alamy Stock Photo:** Heritage Images / The Print Collector (br). **Dreamstime.com:** Johannes Gerhardus Swanepoel (ca). **NASA:** (cr). **172-173 Dreamstime.com:** Micha Rojek / Michalrojek (Background). **172 Dreamstime.com:** Walter Arce (clb). **173 Dreamstime.com:** Solarseven (cr). **NASA:** Johns Hopkins University Applied Physics Laboratory / Southwest Research Institute (bl). **174-175 123RF.com:** Rustyphil (t). **176 123RF.com:** Alexmit (cla). **NASA:** ESA, and the Hubble Heritage Team (STScI / AURA); Acknowledgment: J. Gallagher (University of Wisconsin), M. Mountain (STScI), and P. Puxley (National Science Foundation) (br). **Science Photo Library:** European Southern Observatory (clb). **Shutterstock.com:** Roupplar (cr). **177 Getty Images / iStock:** M-Gucci (tr). **NASA:** JPL-Caltech (c). **178 NASA:** MSFC (r); JSC / Robert Markowitz (bl). **179 Alamy Stock Photo:** NASA / Dembinsky Photo Associates (crb). **Dreamstime.com:** Andrey Armyagov (tl); Grejak (clb). **NASA: (b);** STS-116 Shuttle Crew (cra). **180 Dreamstime.com:** Vasyl Helevachuk (bc); Viktoriia Kasyanyuk (cb); Sarah2 (bc/beetle). **180-181 Dreamstime.com:** Ovydyborets (Stones); Tribalium (Dandelion). **181 Dorling Kindersley:** Natural History Museum, London / Colin Keates (bc). **Dreamstime.com:** Piolka (tr); Smikeymikey1 (cr); Igor Zubkov (tc/Nest). **Getty Images / iStock:** Antagain (tl). **Shutterstock.com:** lukaszemanphoto (br); Unikyluckk (bl); Yulia Tashirova (tc). **182 Dreamstime.com:** Pavel Kudriavtsev (tl). **Getty Images / iStock:** barbol88 (bc). **Shutterstock.com:** Unikyluckk (crb). **183 Dreamstime.com:** Aviag7 (bc); Tony Campbell (cla); Aleksandar Grozdanovski (ca); Markbeckwith (tr); Tribalium (clb); Luayana (cb); Vladvitek (br). **Shutterstock.com:** Deep OV (tl); Gema Alvarez Fernandez (c). **184 Dreamstime.com:** Tunedin61 / Stephan Bock (bl). **185 Alamy Stock Photo:** Alf Jacob Nilsen (cb). **186 Getty Images / iStock:** Merlinpf (bl); TrongNguyen (r). **187 Dorling Kindersley:** Natural History Museum, London / Colin Keates (crb). **Getty Images / iStock:** Demarfa (bl). **Science Photo Library:** Detlev Van Ravenswaay (br). **188 123RF.com:** Keith Levit (cla). **188-189 Dreamstime.com:** Isselee (c); Jesse Kraft. **189 Dorling Kindersley:** Natural History Museum, London / Down House / Dave King (cra). **Dreamstime.com:** Mogens Trolle (crb). **Getty Images / iStock:** Grafissimo (tr). **190-191 Alamy Stock Photo:** BSIP SA / IMAGE POINT FR - LPN (c). **190 Dreamstime.com:** Nchuprin / Andrey Sukhachev (br). **191 Dreamstime.com:** Oleg Kovtun (ca); Norbert Dr. Lange (tl). **Getty Images / iStock:** tonaquatic (br). **Shutterstock.com:** Dotted Yeti (bl). **193 Dreamstime.com:** Decade3d (cla); Sebastian Kaulitzki (ca, **clb);** Christopher Jackson (cra); Kateryna Kon (cb); Maya Kovacheva Photography (br). **195 Alamy Stock Photo:** NASA Photo (crb). **Getty Images / iStock:** ranasu (cr). **196 Dreamstime.com:** Viktoriia Kasyanyuk (b); Piolka (leaves bg); Wabeno (crb). **197 Dreamstime.com:** Chernetskaya (cra). **Getty Images / iStock:** lanolan (ca). **198-199 Depositphotos Inc:** Pakhnyushchyy (t). **Dreamstime.com:** Seamartini (b). **199 Dreamstime.com:** Fedecandoniphoto (tl); Marek Uliasz (tc); Michael Smith (tr); Ovydyborets (cla); Sarah2 (fcl); Vasyl Helevachuk (cl); Volodymyr Tsyba (cr). **Shutterstock.com:** David Calvert (br). **200 Dreamstime.com:** Csourav (tr); Christian Jung (cra). **naturepl.com:** Alex Hyde (bl). **201 Alamy Stock Photo:** Science Photo Library / Steve Gschmeissner (cl). **Dreamstime.com:** Shcl40 (tr); Smikeymikey1 (cr); Ugur Ucan (cb). **202 123RF.com:** Chonlasub Woravichan (bl). **Dreamstime.com:** Defun / Xunbin Pan (cb); Jan Pokorn (ca); Isselee (clb). **203 Dreamstime.com:** Annaav (cra); Fenkieandreas / Fenkie Sumolang (bl); Stu Porter (clb). **Getty Images / iStock:** drakuliren (tc). **204 Dreamstime.com:** Dirk Jan Mattaar (b); Theblueplanet (cla); Nurjanah Nurjanah (clb). **Shutterstock.com:** logistock (br). **204-205 Shutterstock.com:** Yulia Tashirova (tc). **205 Dreamstime.com:** Nuwat Chanthachanthuek (cb); Igor Zubkov (tl); Musat Christian (cl); Hotshotsworldwide (ca); Phant (cr); Marietjie Opperman (br). **206 Alamy Stock Photo:** blueshiftstudios / David Cook (crb); Buiten-Beeld / Jelger Herder (c); Minden Pictures / Jelger Herder / Buiten-beeld (ca). **206-207 Dreamstime.com:** Unweit. **207 Alamy Stock Photo:** Nature & Landscapes / Mikel Bilbao Gorostiaga (tl); Scenics & Science (c); Nature Photographers Ltd / Paul R. Sterry (cb); Steve. Trewhella (crb). **208 123RF.com:** vladsilver (bc). **Depositphotos Inc:** Pakhnyushchyy (clb). **Dreamstime.com:** Chansom Pantip (tl). **Shutterstock.com:** ERainbow (bl); MarcusVDT (c). **209 Dreamstime.com:** Grafner (br); Ygcreativestudio (cra). **Shutterstock.com:** Kseniya Art (cb); Erik Mandre (tl); Pablo Mazorra (cr); Ketan shah (bl). **210 Dreamstime.com:** Anankkml (clb); Isselee (cl); Leigh Prather (bl). **210-211 Getty Images / iStock:** DigitalVision Vectors / JDawnInk (fish silhouette). **211 Alamy Stock Photo:** Arterra Picture Library / Arndt Sven-Erik (tr). **Getty Images / iStock:** E+ / dagsjo (cra). **Shutterstock.com:** zaferkizilkaya (cr). **212 123RF.com:** wizzard (ca). **Dreamstime.com:** Pornsawan Baipakdee (b); Thodoristibilis (br). **Shutterstock.com:** lukaszemanphoto (bc); Bernhard Staehli (tr). **213 123RF.com:** Sirylok (crb). **Dreamstime.com:** Patrimonio Designs Limited (cra); Tartilastock (c). **Shutterstock.com:** sumroeng chinnapan (clb); fish1715 (cla); wim claes (cla/bird); Frank Gaertner (b). **214 Dreamstime.com:** Kittipong Jirasukhanont (br). **215 Dorling Kindersley:** Natural History Museum, London / Philip Dowell (tc). **216 123RF.com:** tobi (plates x4). **Alamy Stock Photo:** D. Hurst (cl). **Dreamstime.com:** Oleg Dudko (cr). **216-217 Dreamstime.com:** Kritchanut (b); Salamatik (t). **217 Dreamstime.com:** Arisa Thepbanchornchai (crb). **218-219 123RF.com:** lattesmile (b). **218 Dreamstime.com:** Petovarga (bl). **220 123RF.com:** leonello calvetti (tc). **220-221 Dreamstime.com:** Wisconsinart (b)

Cover images: *Front:* **Alamy Stock Photo:** Nature & Landscapes / Mikel Bilbao Gorostiaga tc/ (caterpillar); **Dreamstime.com:** Sebastian Kaulitzki bl, Misuhashistock b/ (bg), Nerthuz cla, Konstantin Shaklein cl, Tirrasa cra, Ulkan120 cla/ (cable), Vanda Vasilevskaya (x4), Vlad3563 tc/ (amethyst); **Getty Images / iStock:** VvoeVale tc; *Back:* **123RF.com:** leonello calvetti tl; **Alamy Stock Photo:** Maurice Savage crb/ (robot); **Dreamstime.com:** 64samcorp tc, Chaoss (bg), Costasz tc/ (bottle), Egal / Elena Schweitzer bl, Anton Ignatenco cr, Patrick Marcel Pelz tc/ (recycle), Misuhashistock b/ (bg), Evgenii Naumov cb/ (building), Sergey Novikov tr, Ominaesi crb, Showvector cb, Vanda Vasilevskaya cra, cl; *Spine:* **Dreamstime.com:** Vanda Vasilevskaya t/ (x2)